NOAH'S FLOOD: THE BASICS

Daniel A. Biddle, Ph.D.

Copyright © 2024 by Genesis Apologetics, Inc.
E-mail: staff@genesisapologetics.com

www.genesisapologetics.com
A 501(c)(3) ministry equipping youth pastors, parents, and students with the Biblical truth about Genesis, Creation, and the Flood.

The entire contents of this book (including videos) are available online: *www.noahsflood.com*

Noah's Flood: The Basics

by Daniel A. Biddle, Ph.D.
Printed in the United States of America

ISBN: 9798870087924

All rights reserved solely by the author. The author guarantees all contents are original and do not infringe upon the legal rights of any other person or work. No part of this book may be reproduced in any form without the permission of the author. The views expressed in this book are not necessarily those of the publisher.

Scripture taken from the New King James Version®. Copyright © 1982 by Thomas Nelson. Used by permission. All rights reserved.

Print Version 2024

Download the FREE "Genesis Apologetics" Mobile App for Creation v. Evolution Videos!

Contents

About Genesis Apologetics...5
Introduction...6
What Was the Pre-flood World Like?...8
When was Noah's Flood and How Long Did It Last?..............15
How Could the Ark Have Been Seaworthy?............................17
How Could All the Animals Fit on the Ark?............................19
Flood Legends from Around the World...................................21
How It All Happened: Catastrophic Plate Tectonics...............40
Dinosaur Fossils: Look No Further If You Want Evidence for the Worldwide Flood!..60
Noah's Flood: How Did People and Animals Disperse Around the World after the Flood?..90
Helpful Resources...93
Prayer of Salvation..94
Endnotes..97

About Genesis Apologetics

Genesis Apologetics is a non-profit 501(c)(3) ministry that provides Christians with training programs for students of all ages covering Creation, Noah's Flood, the fossil record, gender sex and marriage, race, evolution, the reliability of the Bible, and others. Our programs have been used in schools around the world, translated into 13 languages, distributed by mainstream Christian outlets, and are available free online:

- *Noah's Flood Movie ("The Ark and the Darkness: Unearthing the Mysteries of Noah's Flood") and Resources:* www.noahsflood.com
- *Foundations Movie:* A free movie that shows just how important it is to believe in God's Word, starting with the very first page: www.foundationsmovie.com
- *Genesis Impact:* A free movie showing an equipped Christian debating a museum docent about the leading evidences for evolution in museums (great for preparing before visiting museums): www.genesisimpact.com
- *Mobile App:* Search *Genesis Apologetics* in App stores.
- *K-8 Students* enjoy our Student Zone: www.genesisapologetics.com/students.
- *5th-10th Graders* can learn from the **Debunking Evolution** program which takes apart the Top 10 pillars of evolution and contrasts them with the truth of Biblical Creation. Six video-based lessons and Student Guide workbook included! www.debunkevolution.com
- *11th-12th Graders* can use our **Debunking the Seven Myths** program to prepare for the Top Seven false teachings about Genesis, Creation, and Flood that they will encounter in college: www.sevenmyths.com
- YouTube Channel (**Genesis Apologetics**).
- Website: www.genesisapologetics.com

Introduction

It was a blazing hot day in Alberta's Dinosaur Provincial Park, a location with one of the largest dinosaur graveyards in the world. My daughter Makaela and I were standing beside an outdoor dinosaur fossil exhibit that featured a hadrosaur (duck-billed dinosaur) right where it had been found, buried by the Flood waters. A father and son stood behind us. The boy pressed the button to play the audio recording from the secular museum. It explained how "millions and millions of years ago" this dinosaur tried to swim across a swollen river during a tropical storm and drowned (somehow along with a 13-mile stretch of other dinosaurs, mammals, and sea life that met the same fate at the same time).

After hearing the explanation, Makaela had her "wake-up" moment. She turned to me—with the two strangers standing just feet away—and gave me five-minute verbal storm about how the secular explanation made no sense whatsoever. We were surrounded by a catastrophic burial stretching at least 13 miles where over 32,000 specimens from 35 species, 34 genera, and 12 families of dinosaurs were obviously entombed by hundreds of feet of mud along with fish, turtles, marsupials, amphibians, and countless clams. It was obvious: this was a massive, watery kill zone where these creatures were buried *by* the very water and mud responsible for their death.

We walked back to the car and the man who overheard my daughter's "my eyes are now opened" speech approached me in the parking lot. Expecting him to confront me about my daughter's "Creationist rant," I was shocked when the very opposite happened. He explained that he grew up as a Christian, but lost his faith while attending college to become a licensed geologist (his current occupation). His next words blew me away: "Your daughter's five-minute explanation about the Flood and the dinosaur fossil record made more sense to me than the explanations I received over several years of studying to become a geologist. I am now returning to my faith…" He went on to explain how the millions of years, evolution, and dinosaur burial evidence never made sense to him given what we see in the fossil record, now especially so after learning more about the biblical framework surrounding dinosaurs.

I had two more "coincidental" meetings with him in different locations over the next two days, where we continued the dialogue about making biblical sense over the fossil record. Who could imagine what a young boy pushing the play button at a museum exhibit could do one hot day in Canada?

Students deserve to know that the Bible presents the true case about earth's past, as well as its future. Secular colleges—and even many Christian colleges—teach that the Bible is not real history. The 18 inches that separate the head from the heart can represent a chasm of faith that is never crossed by many. Today's students want to know: When does the truth begin in the Bible? On the first page? How many pages need to be turned until truth begins?

This book helps answer these very important questions. In fact, we challenge any reader—Christian or not—to study these pages and somehow *not* come away with the belief that the Genesis account of the worldwide Flood is a real, historic event. To make this challenge even easier, this book is very short given what it *could* include, and represents a very distilled list of only the leading, salient evidences of Noah's Flood. The complete list is much, much longer than what's provided in these pages. We pray the Lord opens your eyes to the truth of earth history by revealing that when it comes to the early pages of Genesis, the truth is more terrifying than fiction...

What Was the Pre-flood World Like?

Biblical Creation holds that God created a perfect initial world with no death, no carnivory, and no "survival of the fittest."[1] Further, animals were created to reproduce—just as we observe today—after their "own kind." Creationists also believe that this perfect world held out until it was marred by the sin of Adam and Eve, which brought death, suffering, bloodshed, and disease.[2] Geographically, this pre-Flood world may have had only a single landmass[3] until the Flood broke the continents apart. The Flood occurred 1,656 years after Creation according to English Bible translations.

Biblical creationists have presented many pre-Flood climate models over the years, with many of them called "Canopy Models." While several variants exist, all canopy models interpret the "waters above" (firmament) in Genesis 1:7 as some type of water-based canopy encircling the Earth from the beginning of creation until the Flood. As models of history, these ideas held promise to explain the pre-Flood climate, but they produced problems. For example, meteorologist Dr. Larry Vardiman spent decades at the Institute for Creation Research modeling a pre-Flood vapor canopy. In the end, he found no way for the modeled steam to avoid making earth dangerously hot. While these models and others exist, we ultimately don't know what the pre-Flood world was like because we weren't there. Further, the Bible gives few insights. It does suggest the following features:

- Before the Fall, the atmosphere was *perfect* for sustaining life (Genesis 1:31) and there was no death (Genesis 2:17; Romans 5:12; 1 Corinthians 15:22). This soon ended.
- Earth's atmosphere likely had sunlight and temperature variations within the days and nights (Genesis 3:8).
- Given that Adam and Eve were told to be "fruitful and multiply and fill the earth" (Genesis 1:27; 3:21) and they were "naked and unashamed" before the Fall (Genesis 2:25), it appears they had no need of clothing before the Fall.
- The Flood ruptured earth's land mass. It rearranged continents and pushed up today's mountains (Psalm 104:8).
- Genesis 2:5–6 states, "For the Lord God had not caused it to rain on the earth, and there was no man to till the ground; but

a mist went up from the earth and watered the whole face of the ground." While this may mean that there was no rain until the Flood, this passage is at least clear that God originally used an underground system to water plants. After the Flood, the above-ground system we call the water cycle dominated.

- Because the rainbow was given to mark a new covenant between God and the Earth (to never again Flood the entire earth) (Genesis 9:13), there is the possibility that Earth's climate was changed after (and by) the Flood to allow rainbows.[4] However, God may have used an existing phenomenon as a sign of His covenant.

These insights point to the idea that the pre-Flood world was quite different than the post-Flood world of today. The New Testament also acknowledges this distinction. Second Peter 3:6 says, "by which the world that then existed perished, being flooded with water." The fossils also indicate differences in the pre-Flood.

- Giant land beasts, such as sauropod dinosaurs that grew as large as 115 feet and 200,000 pounds.
- Giant flying reptiles called pterosaurs had over 50-foot wingspans (e.g., *Quetzalcoatlus*).
- Giant dragonflies had 2-1/2 foot wingspans and 17-inch bodies (*Meganeura*).
- Mushrooms grew over 20-feet high (*Prototaxites*).[5]
- Giant millipedes grew over eight feet long (*Arthropleura*).
- Sea lilies (not plants, but Echinoderms) are measured in inches today, but reached over a dozen feet before the Flood.
- Millions or more fossils of shallow marine creatures show that the pre-Flood world had vast (continent-sized) stretches of shallow seas unlike today's deep oceans.

The above list could be much longer; these are just a few examples. Biblical creationists and evolutionists agree that these giant creatures, plants, and habitats existed. Indeed, they are in the fossil record for everyone to evaluate, regardless of the worldview lens through which they are viewed. We also agree that these ancient features existed in a *different version of the Earth*. Evolutionists place it millions of years ago, while Biblical creationists place it before the

Flood, just thousands of years ago. Next, we'll look at some of these creatures more closely.

Giant Flying Reptiles (Pterosaurs)

One of the largest flying reptiles is *Quetzalcoatlus*, which was named after the Mesoamerican feathered serpent god, Quetzalcoatl. Many studies have attempted to estimate this creature's wingspan, with most estimates coming in over 36 feet.[6]

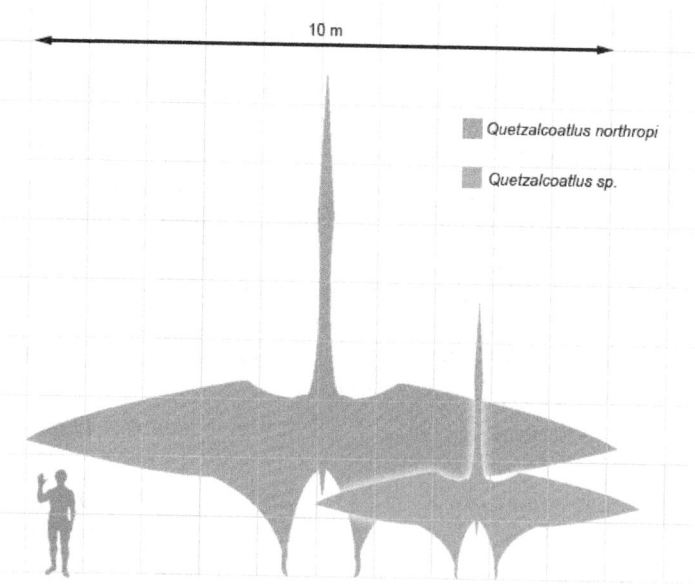

Figure 1. Quetzalcoatlus Wingspan.[7]

The wingspan, however, is not what puzzles scientists about this giant—it's the *large wingspan given its weight*. While estimates vary, some studies estimate the weight of the larger specimens discovered to exceed 500 pounds.[8] That's likely too much weight for a flying creature to bear and still be able to fly. Several studies have investigated how these massive creatures could fly, with some reports even titled, *"This Pterodactyl was so big it couldn't fly"* and opening sentences such as *"Bad news dragon riders: Your dragon can't take off."*[9]

Scientists who have studied and published on this extensively have even admitted: "...it is now generally agreed that even the largest pterosaurs could not have flown in today's skies" and have offered explanations such as "warmer climate" or "higher levels of atmospheric oxygen" as reasons it could have flown only during the era in which it lived.[10]

Some secular studies that have investigated air bubbles trapped in amber that was dated to the "ancient world in which dinosaurs lived," have found *both* increased pressure as well as greater oxygen levels. The magazine *New Scientist* wrote, "One implication is that the atmospheric pressure of the Earth would have been much greater during the Cretaceous Era [rock system], when the bubbles formed in the resin. A dense atmosphere could also explain how the ungainly pterosaur, with its stubby body and wing span of up to 11 meters, could have stayed airborne."[11]

Giant Dragonflies (Meganeura)

The largest dragonfly species alive today (*Megaloprepus caerulatus*) has a wingspan of up to seven inches and a body up to five inches long. Based on the fossil record, the largest pre-Flood dragonflies (*Meganeura*) had wingspans up to 2-1/2 feet and a 17-inch body. See Figure 2.

Figure 2. Giant Pre-Flood Dragonfly (*Meganeura*).[12]

In October 2006, *Science Daily* publicized a study led by Arizona State University staff titled "Giant Insects Might Reign if Only There Was More Oxygen in the Air."[13] The article claims:

> The delicate lady bug in your garden could be frighteningly large if only there was a greater concentration of oxygen in the air, a new study concludes. The study adds support to the theory that some insects were much larger during the late Paleozoic period because they had a much richer oxygen supply, said the study's lead author Alexander Kaiser. The Paleozoic period…was a time of huge and abundant plant life and rather large insects—dragonflies had two-and-a-half-foot wing spans, for example. The air's oxygen content was 35% during this period, compared to the 21% we breathe now, Kaiser said.

This research lends evidence to the fact that the pre-Flood world was different than the one we live in today.

One study conducted in 2010 by researchers at Arizona State University tested this "more oxygen = bigger insects" theory directly by raising 12 different types of insects in simulated atmospheres with various oxygen levels. Their study included three sets of 75 dragonflies in atmospheres containing 12%, 21%, and 31% oxygen levels and their experiment confirmed that dragonflies grow bigger with more oxygen.[14]

A host of reasons could explain why the pre-Flood dragonflies grew much larger than even those in the experiment. They probably had not yet lost the genetics for large size, oxygen could have been a limiting factor (as the body of the insect grows larger, the mass grows faster than the surface area, making it harder to intake enough oxygen for the needs of the body the larger it grows). We also know that creatures lived longer before the flood.

Giant Mushrooms (Prototaxites) and Plants

You don't need to read many secular-based books about the "ancient Earth" before learning about gigantic vegetation that existed supposedly millions of years ago. One example is the *Prototaxites* (see Figure 3). Some reports even state that these gigantic (now extinct) mushroom-like plants covered much of the Earth and "dotted the ancient landscape."[15]

Figure 3. *Prototaxites*

First discovered by a Canadian in 1859, no one seemed to know what they were. But after 130 years of debate whether this plant was a lichen, fungus, or some kind of tree, scientists have come to some level of agreement that it was essentially a "gigantic early mushroom."

Plants and fungi like these puzzle evolutionists, such as Kevin Boyce of Geophysical Sciences at University of Chicago, who stated, "A 20-foot tall fungus doesn't make any sense. Neither does a 20-foot tall algae make any sense, but here's the fossil."[16]

From a Biblical creation standpoint, this is simply a gigantic pre-Flood fungus that God created. It could thrive in the pre-Flood world, but not now. In a temperate, pre-Flood world where wearing clothing was (originally) "optional," it's no wonder that giant fungus and plants like this could have thrived.

Giant Millipedes (Arthropleura)

Giant millipedes (called *Arthropleura*) that grew to be over eight feet long[17] used to crawl around before the Flood in what became northeastern America and Scotland. The larger species of this group are the largest known land invertebrates of all time. Evolutionists attribute their grand size to different pressures and/or oxygen levels of Earth's ancient past.[18]

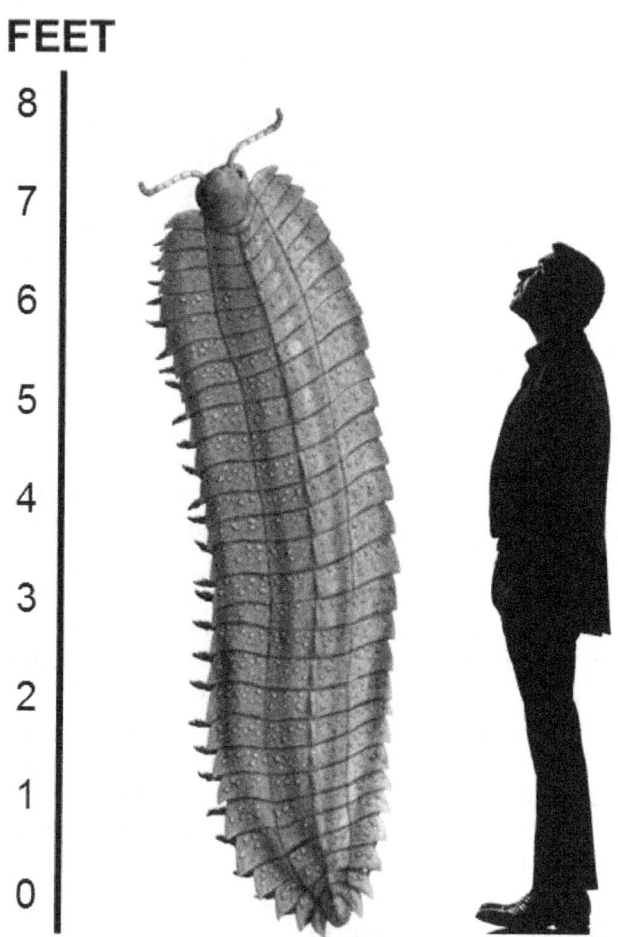

Figure 4. Giant pre-Flood Millipedes (*Arthropleura*).

When was Noah's Flood and How Long Did It Last?

A straight-forward reading from today's modern bibles places Noah's Flood about 2,348 BC. This classic timeline comes from the 17th-century historian Bishop James Ussher, who used the biblical genealogies and other sources to estimate the year of Creation at 4,004 BC.

Some recent research into the copyist differences in the early Masoretic text (the primary source used for our Bibles today) and early Septuagint texts (early Greek translation of the Old Testament) place the Flood around 2,518 BC based on the Masoretic text and between 3,158 BC and 3,298 BC based on the Septuagint (and other early texts), with Creation as early as 5,554 BC.[19] None of these differences, however, tarnish the perfect nature of the *original writings* which were "written through man by God" without error. These issues have been discussed in leading creation journals and readers are encouraged to study this topic further.

So, how long did the Flood last? Genesis 6–9 includes a diary from the very people who went through the Flood, including how the Flood started, major milestones during the process, to how it ended. Table 1 summarizes the entire process.

Table 1. Flood Duration (Adopted from Answers in Genesis[20])

Timeline (days)	Duration	Month/Day	Description	Bible Reference
0	Initial reference point	600th year of Noah's life: 2nd month, 17th day of the month	The fountains of the great deep broke apart and the windows of heaven were opened on the 17th day of the 2nd month. Noah actually entered the Ark seven days prior to this.	Genesis 7:11
40	40 days and nights	3rd month, 27th day of the month	Rain fell for 40 days, then water covered the earth's highest places (at that time) by over ~20 feet and began the stage of flooding until the next milestone.	Genesis 7:11–12, Genesis 7:17–20
150	150 days (including	7th month, 17th day of the month	Water rose to highest level (covering the whole earth) between day 40-150, and the	Genesis 7:24–8:5

15

	the initial 40 days)		end of these 150 days was the 17th day of the 7th month. Ark rested on the mountains of Ararat. Springs of the deep stop on day 150, rain ceased, and the water began receding.	
150 + 74 = 224	74 days	10th month, 1st day of the month	The tops of the mountains became visible on the first day of the 10th month.	Genesis 8:5
224 + 40 = 264	40 days	11th month, 11th day of the month	After 40 more days, Noah sent out a raven.	Genesis 8:6
264 + 7 = 271	7 days	11th month, 18th day of the month	The dove was sent out 7 days after the raven. Returned after finding no resting place.	Genesis 8:6–12
271 + 7 = 278	7 days	11th month, 25th day of the month	After 7 more days, Noah sent out the dove again, returning this time with an olive leaf in its beak.	Genesis 8:10–11
278 + 7 = 285	7 days	12th month, 2nd day of the month	After 7 more days, Noah sent out the dove again, and it did not return.	Genesis 8:12
314	29 days	601st year of Noah life: 1st month, 1st day of the month	Noah removed the cover of the Ark on the 1st day of the 1st month. Earth's *surface* was dried up from Noah's perspective.	Genesis 8:13
370 (371 if counting the first day and last day as full days)	56 days	2nd month, 27th day of the month	The *earth* was dry, and God commanded Noah's family and the animals to exit. From the 1st day of the year during the daylight portion there were 29.5 more days left in the month plus 26.5 more days left in the 2nd month until the exit	Genesis 8:14–17, Genesis 7:11

How Could the Ark Have Been Seaworthy?

Let's investigate whether the Ark was seaworthy. God gave certain dimensions to Noah for building the Ark: 300 cubits long, 50 cubits wide, and 30 cubits high. Using the Nippur Cubit[21] at 20.4 inches, this works out to a vessel about 510 feet long, 85 feet wide, and 51 feet high. Accounting for a 15% reduction in volume due to the hull curvature, the Ark had about 1.88 million cubic feet of space, the equivalent of 450 semi-trailers of cargo space.[22] Twice as long as a Boeing 747 and stretching over one-and-a-half football fields, this was a massive ship.

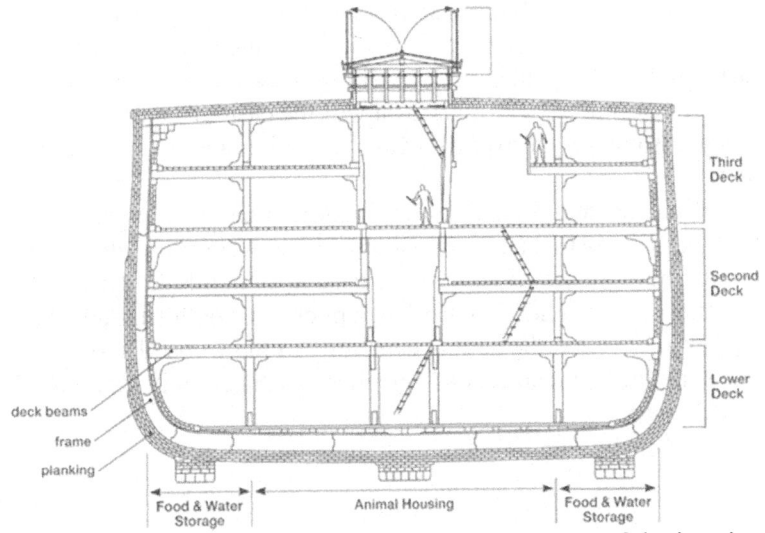

Figure 5. Cross-sectional view of a possible design of the interior of the ark.[23]

God knew *exactly what He was doing* when He gave Noah the specific dimensions of the Ark. In 1993, Dr. Seon Won Hong conducted a scientific study[24] to investigate the seaworthiness of the Ark at the renowned ship research center KRISO (now called MOERI) in South Korea.[25] After evaluating the seaworthiness of over 10 various ship dimensions, the study showed that the Ark dimensions given in the Bible were ideal for handling everything a highly turbulent sea could throw at it, while balancing the need for

17

inhabitant safety. The study showed that the Ark could handle 100-foot waves.

An earlier study conducted in the 17th Century by Peter Jansen of Holland showed that the length-to-width ratio of the Ark (about 7-to-1) was ideal for such a massive, non-powered sea vessel. Some oil tankers have a 7-to-1 ratio as well. He also demonstrated using replica models of the Ark how tough it was to capsize.[26]

Noah was instructed by God to coat the inside and the outside of the Ark with pitch, a thick gooey substance secreted by trees as a means of protection against infection or insect attack. Isn't it interesting that one of the very first historical references to using pitch for ships is in the Bible? It's also interesting that pitch has been the most effective and widely-used ship waterproofing substance in history. For centuries, tar, which is made from pitch, was among Sweden's most important exports, peaking at over a quarter million barrels per year in the late 1800s. Many of the eastern states in the U.S. were also major tar exporters for ship building purposes until the 1900s.[27]

When heated into a liquid state and applied to ship planking, pitch hardens almost instantly into a protective, waterproof shell, very similar to how epoxy or fiberglass are used in shipbuilding today. The strong outer shell provided by hardened pitch adds both strength and waterproofing beyond the natural capability of the wood. These "divine shipbuilding instructions" given to Noah certainly seem to make realistic sense.

How Could All the Animals Fit on the Ark?

One of the most frequently asked questions about the Ark is: "How could it fit all the animals?" Two factors help answer this question: (1) the size of the Ark, and (2) the number (and size) of the animals and supplies on board. First, the size. Given the size of the Ark (discussed above), the Ark had a total volume of at least 1,396,000 cubic feet.[28] The inside dimensions of a 40-foot school bus gives about 2,080 cubic feet of space. Therefore, at least 671 school buses without their wheels and axels could fit inside of Noah's Ark. If each bus carried 50 students, then 33,550 kids could easily fit in the Ark.

Next, we have the number of animals. The Genesis Flood account states that God brought two (male/female) of every *kind* of air-breathing, land-dwelling animal (and seven pairs of some) to Noah, who loaded them into the Ark. The Hebrew term for kind is *min*, which occurs only 31 times in the Old Testament. So just what is a biblical kind? Biblically and biologically speaking, a kind is a group of animals that were naturally interfertile at the time of the Flood. Some organisms have complex histories since then, so it's difficult to determine which of them belongs to which kind. Most often, however, plants and animals interbreed within their modern "Family" classification. Thus, each family—give or take—had at least two representatives on Noah's ark. Several creation scientists have spent considerable amount of time studying this very topic (it's called the field of *baraminology*, or the study of "created kinds").[29]

While there are various methods for determining "kinds," (e.g., cognitum and statistical baraminology), hybridization (whether two species can have offspring) is considered the most valuable evidence for inclusion within an Ark *kind*. Take mammals for example. Some biologists list them in 28 orders that include 146 families and over 4,800 species.[30] Some place the species estimates higher, around 5,400.[31] So how many different mammal pairs would Noah have to take on the Ark to produce all the mammal species we have today? Take the dog (Canine) kind for starters. The World Canine Organization currently recognizes 339 different breeds of dogs—all are or were interfertile. There are 335 horse breeds that are all interfertile. There are eight bear species in the bear (Ursidae) family and all except for one are interfertile. Notice how the high number of species quickly collapses to a much smaller number?

Figure 6. Ursidae Family (Bears).

Some scientists have boiled down this list of mammal species to only 138 created kinds (using extant species, or animals still alive today). Including the extinct mammalian families known from the fossil record, the actual number on the Ark could have exceeded 300.[32] By collapsing the other animal categories in a similar manner, the total estimate of the number of kinds needed on the Ark is fewer than 2,000.[33] Dinosaurs were certainly included on the ark, since Scripture says any animal that walked and had nostrils went in, with many dinosaur count estimates at the species level less than 1,000 and fewer than 80 at the family level.[34] Noah's family could have loaded young behemoths, not the larger older ones. Dinosaur kinds, plus many other animals, went extinct after the Flood.

Flood Legends from Around the World

If the Biblical Flood really happened and the descendants of the Flood survivors were spread around the globe at the Babel event shortly after the Flood, we would expect to find flood legends preserved in the 70+ groups dispersed from Babel. The Flood would have been such a significant event that each group would have developed strong oral (and later written) traditions to keep this important part of history alive.

In addition to this, we would expect that the Flood account would change over time, with only some of the main points preserved through the generations. Much like the game of telephone—where information distorts when shared from person to person—we would expect the Flood account to change over time. This is exactly what happened with the Biblical Flood account. So, rather than the differences between the various Flood legends around the world discrediting the Flood account, these differences actually *support* the Flood as a real, historic event.

In his book titled, *Echoes of Ararat: A Collection of Over 300 Flood Legends from North and South America* (2021), Nick Liguori summarizes over 300 legends from people groups around the world that provides overwhelming support to this massive "worldwide telephone game."

Genesis vs. Flood Myths from the Ancient Near East (ANE)

In addition to the Epic of Gilgamesh (covered separately below), the Ancient Near East has five primary Flood accounts that echo the original, Biblical version. These include: the Enuma Elish[35] (about 1,100 BC), Simmonds Ark Tablet[36] (1,700 BC), the Sumerian Kings List[37] (2,000 BC), Atrahasis Epic[38] (1,800 BC), and the Eridu Tablet[39] (1,600 BC).

Something *amazing* emerges when comparing these Flood accounts to the Biblical one: Eight of the main features of the Biblical account are included in each! See Figure 7 below.

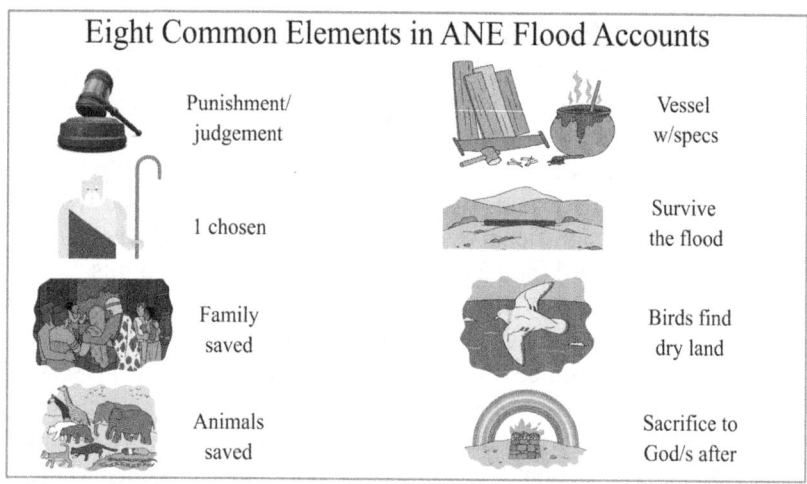

Figure 7. Eight Common Elements in the Ancient Near East Flood Accounts.

Some of these accounts talk about God or "gods" punishing man and one man being chosen to bring either himself or his family to safety and (in every case) all the animals onto a vessel to survive the flood. Afterward we have
various details about this chosen man sending a dove or a raven (just like the Biblical text). When the person gets off the Ark, in almost every story he offers a sacrifice to please God or "gods." While many of these elements are not in the same chronological order as the Bible's account, they include the same unique events and similar major details.

While all these accounts pre-date the *version* of the Bible that we possess today, the Bible comes across more historical and more believable. While these myths are complex and they differ in the details, where they *all* agree is the similar core history that must have been passed on after the Flood. As civilization spread and generations began to go their own way, they developed their own myths which kept that common history but added to it in their own ways.

The Bible, on the other hand, doesn't do it that way. The Bible's account is not a perception, but rather the writer is saying, "this is the way it happened" and it's laid out in an orderly fashion. The Bible provides historical timeframes, genealogies of all the key players before and after the Flood, and clear, feasible dimensions of the Ark that are quite literal and actually work. The Bible lays out exact dimensions of something that is hydrodynamically stable and large enough for boarding all animal kinds.

By contrast, the other flood myths include strange, unfeasible ark proportions (like a square box or a round basket), timelines that are unreasonable, and other characteristics of the Biblical account that are re-framed as exaggerations. It's clear these storytellers have the idea of a boat, but they're too far from the source information and they tended to exaggerate and change their own versions of the story.

The Bible vs. the Epic of Gilgamesh

When comparing the Genesis Flood to the Epic of Gilgamesh, several clues point to the Biblical account being the *original, historical* account. First, the 12 tablets of the Epic of Gilgamesh we have today were found in 1853 and dated to around 650 BC, although parts of the story existed in earlier, fragmentary versions.[40] Because the story had many of the same elements as the Genesis account, skeptics believed that Gilgamesh preceded the Biblical account, negating the Genesis account as just a spin-off. Fortunately for Christians, however, there are major clues that point to the Biblical account as the accurate one, and Gilgamesh as a later work of fiction that incorporated legendary elements of a flood within a cultural fantasy. Here are the reasons why.

First, we have the feasibility of the Gilgamesh version of the Ark, described as a massive, unstable cube that was about 200 feet on each side with six decks that divided it into seven parts. Gilgamesh supposedly built this vessel—which was over three times the size of the Biblical Ark, in just a week. How would something like this fare during a worldwide Flood? It would obviously tumble, killing or maiming its passengers. That's obviously quite different than the biblical Ark which had a 7-to-1 length-to-width ratio which is very similar to many of today's ocean barges, making it a feasible design for staying afloat during the Flood. Scripture provides clues that Noah and helpers took over 55 years to build the Ark.[41]

The second key for determining which of these Flood accounts is the original is the *duration* of the Flood provided by each. The Gilgamesh flood lasted a mere six days, whereas the Genesis Flood lasted 371 days. Both accounts claim the Flood was worldwide, but how could water cover earth in just six days? A floating 200-foot cube and six days for worldwide inundation certainly stretch credulity.

The next consideration is the reasons for the Flood given by each of the two accounts. In the Genesis account, God's judgment is *just*—he was patient with utterly wicked mankind for 120 years before sending the Flood and showed mercy to the last righteous family. In the Gilgamesh account, the Flood was ordered by multiple, self-centered squabbling 'gods' that were 'starving' without humans to feed them sacrifices. These two are quite different!

Finally, there are several other parts of the Gilgamesh account that are obviously mythical, such as Gilgamesh being 2/3rds divine and 1/3rd mortal. After oppressing his people, Gilgamesh and others call upon the 'gods' and the sky-god Anu creates a wild man named Enkidu to fight Gilgamesh. The battle is a draw, and they become friends. Gilgamesh apparently also encounters talking monsters and a "Scorpion man" in his journeys.

These stark differences between Genesis and Gilgamesh accounts highlight the feasibility and priority of the biblical one. The Gilgamesh account was written 800 years[42] *after* Genesis and describes a cube-shaped Ark 200 feet on each side tumbling around in the ocean in a six-day flood put on by the "angry, fighting gods" that sent it. The Bible's Flood was recorded earlier, has an Ark sealed on the inside and out with dimensions that are on par with today's ocean liners, lasted a full year, and was sent to judge an Earth that deserved it.

Many myths are based on historical accounts, but they get embellished over time, becoming more and more imaginative as the story is repeated over generations. This is exactly what we see with flood myths like Gilgamesh—they take the original, historical account (the Biblical Flood) and grow it into a mythical, fantastic story over time.

For example, the earlier version of the Gilgamesh Flood account[43] clearly identifies the flood as a local river flood, with the dead bodies of humans filling the river "like dragonflies" and moving to the edge of the boat "like a raft" and moving to the riverbank "like a raft." Centuries later, this gets exaggerated into a global, worldwide flood where humans killed in the flood "fill the sea" like a "spawn of fish."

Both accounts have a God or "gods" that are sending judgment, describe a worldwide inundation, have an Ark built to specific dimensions that are loaded with surviving humans and animals, and land just a few hundred miles apart from each other after using birds as a test to find dry land. Myths often grow from historical to being more mythical, but they almost never develop in the reverse, becoming more truthful and accurate over time. While these accounts mirror each other in so many ways, which account is the original, historical one? The feasible one, of course. While both accounts describe plenty of divine intervention, only the Biblical ark size, shape, function, build time, and flood duration makes sense.

Table 2 provides a comparison between the Genesis Flood Account and the Epic of Gilgamesh by looking at 24 different characteristics of each. A careful study reveals the Genesis account as the feasible, historical one, and the Gilgamesh account as the mythical one that is several steps removed from the original, Biblical account.

Table 2. Comparison between Genesis and Gilgamesh.[44]

Comparison of Genesis and Gilgamesh		
FACTOR	GENESIS	GILGAMESH
Extent of flood	Global	Global
Cause	Man's wickedness	Man's sins
Intended for whom?	All mankind	One city & all mankind
Sender	Yahweh	Assembly of "gods"
Name of hero	Noah	Utnapishtim
Hero's character	Righteous	Righteous
Means of announcement	Direct from God	In a dream
Ordered to build boat?	Yes	Yes
Did hero complain?	Yes	Yes
Height of boat	Several stories (3)	Several stories (6)
Compartments inside?	Many	Many
Doors	One	One
Windows	At least one	At least one
Outside coating	Pitch	Pitch
Shape of boat	Rectangular	Square
Human passengers	Family members only	Family & few others
Other passengers	All species of animals	All species of animals
Means of flood	Ground water & heavy rain	Heavy rain
Duration of flood	Long (371 days)	Short (6 days & nights)
Test to find land	Release of birds	Release of birds
Types of birds	Raven & three doves	Dove, swallow, raven
Ark landing spot	Mountain -- Mt. Ararat	Mountain -- Mt. Nisir
Sacrificed after flood?	Yes, by Noah	Yes, by Utnapishtim
Blessed after flood?	Yes	Yes

Flood Legends from North and South America

Nick Liguori summarizes over 300 legends from indigenous tribes that provide overwhelming support to this massive, worldwide "telephone game" when it comes to the Flood. He summarizes his findings by stating:

> We have heard the testimony of over 300 tribes from North and South America. From the Ute people of the slopes of the Rockies, to the jungles of South America—from the Inuit people of northern Arctic coasts, to the Yaghan tribes of the southernmost parts of the hemisphere—all of these tribes have given their testimony. Although their stories differ in many ways, they all agree on the fact that a great flood happened long ago. When we examine the recurring details—the forewarning (almost always given to an old man), the great canoe, the saving of pairs of animals, the landing on a high mountain, the raven and the dove sent in search of land, the freshly plucked leaf, the sacrifice, the rainbow, and the godless ways of man that provoked the Flood—they all match those of the Genesis Flood account.

Drilling deeper into these flood legends reveals that 18 of the North American Flood traditions confirm the Genesis account regarding the raven and dove being sent, with the dove returning with a fresh leaf in its beak, 20 agree with Genesis regarding the cause of the Flood (God's judgement upon man's evil ways), and 27 agree with Genesis that the ark was canoe-like in shape.[45] Liguori also points out that *zero* of the legends agree with the Epic of Gilgamesh versions on these same details, further indicating the Bible as the real, historical version. Isn't it amazing that groups separated by thousands of miles preserved such similarities to the original Genesis account?

Let's take a tour through Liguori's "Top 10" list from these 300+ native flood legends[46]:

1) Mandan (North Dakota): In the 1830s, George Catlin stood in amazement as he was privileged to watch the annual ceremony of the Mandan tribe of North Dakota. This ceremony, which the

Mandan have solemnly observed since ancient times, vividly preserved the memory of Nu-mohkmunk-a-nah, "the only man," the Noah of the Mandan tribe. This man, they told, survived the flood and landed his big canoe on a mountain far to the west. This elaborate ritual demonstrated a memory of the flood very similar to the Genesis account even to several details. For example, Catlin described the "bull dance," which was performed 40 times during this ceremony, "the exact number of days that it rained upon the earth, according to the Mosaic account." The Mandans also highly esteemed the turtle dove, which they say returned to their Noah carrying a willow bough in its mouth as a sign of the retreating waters.

2) Hualapai (Arizona): The Hualapai possess ancient rock carvings at Spirit Mountain, long predating the arrival of Europeans, which recount the flood and depict eight survivors. They narrate the history thus: "Rains fell on the earth for 45 days. The rising waters wiped out all peoples with the lone exception of an old man atop Spirit Mountain." Then a bird was sent out, and on its second flight it returned "with grass in its beak to inform the man that the waters had receded." This remarkably matches what Genesis says: "again he [Noah] sent the dove out from the ark. Then the dove came to him in the evening, and behold, a freshly plucked olive leaf was in her mouth; and Noah knew that the waters had receded from the earth" (Genesis 8:10–11).

3) Cochiti (a pueblo people of New Mexico): The Cochiti told that a great boat was built and that "they began to load it with much corn and they took all the different animals into the boat with a white pigeon." After the rains stopped, the chief said, "We will send the white pigeon to see if the earth is uncovered again." The pigeon returned carrying a flower, taken as a sign that the flood was ending. Additional details (from *Echoes of Ararat*) include: "Long ago the people knew that there would be a great flood. Up in the north among the high mountains they built a great boat. When it was nearly time for the water to rise, they began to load it with much corn and they took all the different animals into the boat and a white pigeon. When everything was ready the sons of the builder of the boat and their sons came into the ship. When they were all in, they put pitch all over the cracks of the boat. The

flood came. The boat floated on the water. The people that were left on the earth fled to the highest mountain to try to escape from the waters. The ones who could not get to the high mountains were all drowned and floated about on the waters of the flood. The ones who climbed the mountains were overtaken by the water and turned into rocks. Some were embracing each other, and some held one another on their laps, and there they are still just as the water overtook them. Every living thing on the earth was drowned, but the boat still floated. When the waters went down, the boat grounded on a high place in the mountains to the north. Then they knew the waters were subsiding. The chief said to the rest, "We will send the white pigeon to see if the earth is uncovered again." The white pigeon was let out. At last he returned and told the chief, I have seen the earth and the water has gone down. But it is a terrible thing to see. The people are all drowned and their bodies piled upon the ground." In the boat there was also a crow as white as the pigeon. They sent out the crow to look over the earth. She went out and saw the earth as the pigeon had. But she flew down to the dead bodies and began to pick out their eyes. When she came back to the boat, they knew she had done mischief. They said to her, "What is it that you have done when you were out flying over the earth?" You were white and now your feathers are all black." Again they let the pigeon out to see if the earth was firm again. She went out and as she was flying she saw a flower in blossom. She picked the flower for a sign that the earth was getting firm again, and she took it back to the boat. She said to the owner of the boat, "The plants are all growing again, and I settled on the ground and did not sink into the mud. This flower is a sign of the growing of the plants." So the people on the boat were saved from the first-ending-of-the-world-by-flood."

4) Yakama (Washington State): The Yakama spoke of a great flood that came, "one time in the early suns, back near the beginning." Mankind provoked the Creator with their evil ways, but a good man received a word from God that a flood was coming. "I have heard from the Land Above, the land of the spirits, that a big water is coming—a water that will cover all the land. Make a boat for the good people. Let the bad people be killed by the water." So they made a boat out of the largest cedar tree, and the good

people were saved. Another related quote provided in *Echoes of Ararat* include: "When the earliest missionaries came among the Spokanes, Nez Perces, and Cayuses, who with the Yakimas live in the eastern part of the Territory, they found that those Indians had their tradition of a flood, in which one man and wife were saved on a raft. Each of those three tribes also, together with the Flathead tribes, has their separate Ararat in connection with this event" (Myron Eells, ca. 1877).

5) Ottawa (Canada): The Ottawa, around the year 1770, told the fur trader Alexander Henry about their ancestor Nanibojou, their "Noah," who "lived originally toward the going down of the sun, where being warned, in a dream, that the inhabitants would be drowned by a general flood, produced by heavy rains, he built a raft, on which he afterward preserved his own family, and all the animal world without exception. According to his dream, the rains fell, and a flood ensued. His raft drifted for many moons, during which no land was discovered. Liguori points out: Notice the similarity to the Mandan tradition, among many others. Those who would say "this tradition is inauthentic, the product of missionary influence" are confronted with the difficulty of explaining why these traditions are consistent amongst themselves. The general point is this: Aboriginal traditions of the flood match Genesis on various points, but they also contain their own local peculiarities: a woman who came from the sky, or a muskrat that was sent diving for earth, or a quarrel that started the flood, or a trickster. And when we find these peculiarities *consistently* among tribes of a given region, or of a common language family, these peculiarities point to their genuineness. Skeptics likewise cannot account for the very early date that many of these were collected, that many occur in writing or in petroglyphs, and that, indeed, in other parts of the world they predate both the Christian era and Christ Himself.

6) Toltecs (Mexico): The Toltecs had historical paintings and traditions that told of an ancient flood, which they said occurred 1716 years after the creation of the world (this is within 100 years of the biblical timeframe). Only a few escaped the flood, floating inside a "toplipetlacali," an enclosed vessel. After the flood, they said that "men multiplied and made a very high zacuali ... which

means the highest tower, at which they sought to find shelter when the Second World would be destroyed. In time, the languages were changed and, not understanding each other, the people went to different parts of the world." They said they arrived in Mexico "520 years after the flood had passed, which are five ages." Regarding the various Mexican nations having paintings of the flood, Alexander de Humboldt states: "Of the different nations that inhabit Mexico, paintings representing the deluge of Coxcox are found among the Aztecks, the Miztecks, the Zapotecks, the Tlascaltecks, and the Mechoacanese. The Noah, Xisuthrus, or Menou of these nations, is called Coxcox, Teo-Cipactli, or Tezpi. He saved himself conjointly with his wife, Xochiquetzel, in a bark, or, according to other traditions, on a raft of "ahuahuete" (*Cupressus disticha*). The painting represents Coxcox in the midst of the water, lying in a bark. The mountain, the summit of which, crowned by a tree, rises above the waters, is the Peak of Colhuacan, the Ararat of the Mexicans. The horn, which is represented on the left, is the phonetic hieroglyphic of Colhuacan. At the foot of the mountain appear the heads of Coxcox and his wife. ... The men born after the deluge were dumb: a dove, from the top of a tree, distributes among them tongues, represented under the form of small commas. We must not confound this dove with the bird which brings Coxcox tidings that the waters were dried up. The people of Mechoacan preserved a tradition, according to which Coxcox, whom they called Tezpi, embarked in a spacious "acalli" with his wife, his children, several animals, and grain, the preservation of which was of importance to mankind. When the great spirit, Tezcatlipoca, ordered the waters to withdraw, Tezpi sent out from his bark a vulture, the "zopilote" (*Vultur aura*). This bird, which feeds on dead flesh, did not return on account of the great number of carcasses, with which the earth, recently dried up, was strewed. Tezpi sent out other birds, one of which, the hummingbird alone, returned, holding in its beak a branch covered with leaves. Tezpi, seeing that fresh verdure began to clothe the soil, quitted his bark near the mountain of Colhuacan."

7) Aztecs (Mexico): The Aztecs too have ancient paintings that depict the flood, showing one couple safely floating inside a hollow tree as the world was destroyed by water. In another

ancient pictorial manuscript from Mexico (Codex Vaticanus 3733), we find the depiction of a woman talking to a serpent and two children behind the serpent, contending with each other. The similarity of this painting to Genesis is obvious, and it is confirmed by the literature and traditions from Mexico. As Humboldt explains, the woman is Cihuacohuatl, the "woman of our flesh," and the "serpent woman." She is considered the mother of the human race, and she is "always represented with a great serpent." She is considered the mother of two twin children. She is also considered to have "fallen from her first state of happiness and innocence." Notice that Eve appears in many tribes' traditions, here as talking with a serpent. In other nations' traditions, we get a glimpse of her as falling from heaven for having sinned, in others as being tempted by a serpent or a monster, in others as causing the flood, in others as being bit by a snake. We have many traditions not only of the flood, but of Creation, the Garden of Eden and the Fall, Cain and Abel, and the Tower of Babel.

8) Panama: The natives of Panama told the earliest Spanish colonizers that "when the Flood occurred, a man escaped in a canoe, with his wife and sons, and that from him the people of the world multiplied." This comes from a record from the 1500s, quoted by Herrera in his work Décadas (1601). Other data from Central America: A record of an interview in 1528 attests to the native Nicaraguans' knowledge of the ancient flood too. The Kuna and Guaymi recall the divine judgment by which "all the evil of the world was washed away by the flood," when God "destroyed it with water, and killed all the people," while taking care to "preserve the seed of man."

9) Taino and Carib people (Caribbean Islands): The native tribes of the Caribbean Islands also have their flood traditions, recorded as early as 1493 by Columbus' companions. "The Master of Spirits," said the Caribs, "became angry at the Caribs of that time who were very wicked." So he sent the flood, from which only a few managed to survive. They have a memory of the serpent in the garden of Eden as well. Of the Taino people of Cuba, Juan de Torquemada wrote, "The old people, of more than 70 and 80 years, back when our people [the Spanish] first came to that

island, said that an old man, knowing that the flood was to come, made a great boat. He placed inside it many animals, along with his family. He sent out a raven, which did not return, because it ate from the dead floating corpses. Then he sent a dove, which returned singing and carrying a twig with a leaf."

10) Tamanacs (Venezuela): The tribes along the great Orinoco River in Venezuela have preserved the memory that "at the time of the great waters, when their fathers were forced to have recourse to boats, to escape the general inundation, the waves of the sea beat against the rocks of Encaramada." After taking recourse to boats, they add that "a man and a woman saved themselves on a high mountain, called Tamanacu," and that after the flood they threw palm fruits behind them, which produced men and women, who repopulated the world." This tradition is not limited to the Tamanacs, but it "makes part of a system of historical tradition, of which we find scattered notions among the Maypures of the great cataracts; among the Indians of the Rio Erevato, which runs in to the Caura; and among almost all the tribes of the Upper Orinoco." "Hieroglyphic figures are often seen at great heights, on rocky cliffs," Humboldt added, which memorialize this flood and how the survivors repopulated the earth. Notice that "Missionary influence" doesn't really work when you have rock carvings and persistent traditions across many tribes over a vast area.

Flood Legends from China

China is *rich* with Flood history. Not only is there an obvious Genesis connection in the actual content of their word pictures used in their early writing, there is a true abundance of flood legends from most areas in China. Let's take a tour through both of these sources of evidence.

Ancient Chinese Writing and the Genesis Connection

The oldest Chinese writing we still have today is found on bones called *oracle bones*. The ancient writers recording Chinese history on these bones had an *obvious* connection to Genesis. For example, the ancient Chinese word *boat* is composed of symbols meaning "vessel," "eight," (note there were eight people on the Ark) and "mouths." Ethel Nelson documents the amazing Genesis-Chinese language connection in the works titled *The Discovery of Genesis* and *Oracle Bones Speak*. Institute for Creation Research (ICR) writer Dr. James Johnson highlights some of these key connections in his article "Genesis in Chinese Pictographs."[47]

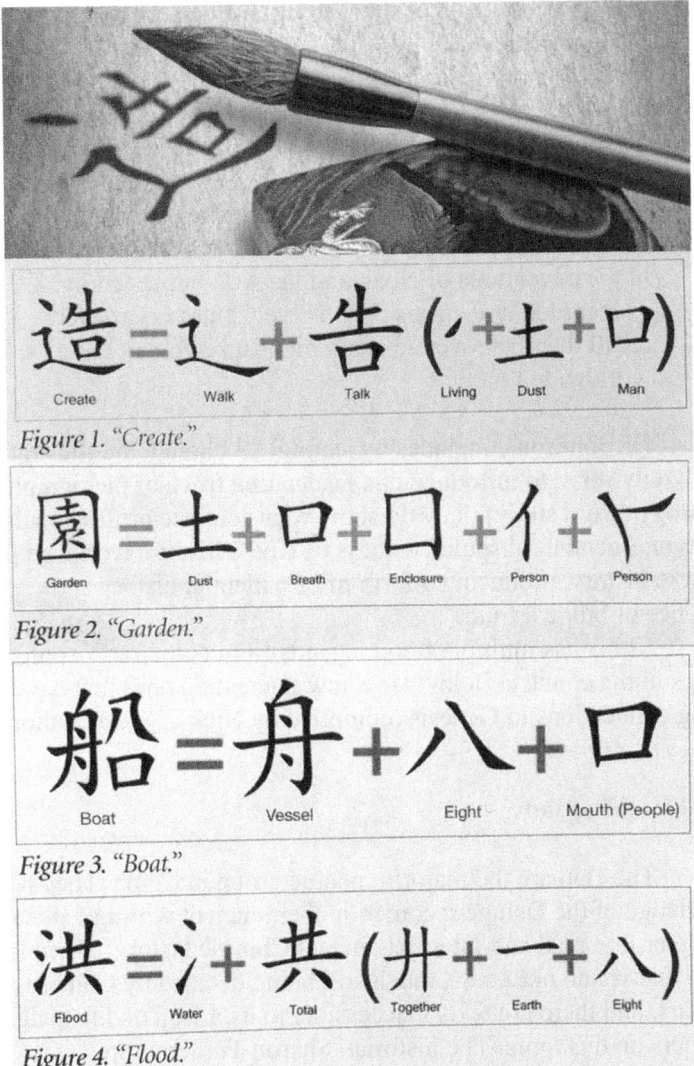

Figure 8. Genesis Origins of Chinese Pictographic Words.

Dr. Johnson summarizes this stunning connection below:

> The pictographic word for "to create" in ancient Chinese is composed of the components "to speak/talk" and "walking"—consistent with the Genesis account of God using His mouth to create and Adam being created fully mature and thus able to walk. Recollection of the Garden of Eden is also evident in the ancient Chinese word for "garden." If this does not link to the Genesis account, why else would the early Chinese combine the ideas of "two persons" who received the "breath" of life after the first one of those two persons (Adam) was made from the "dust" of the earth? The pictographic characters for "boat" and "flood" recall information recounted in the adventures of Noah and his Ark–borne family, as recorded in Genesis 6–9. These Chinese characters recall that there were exactly eight survivors of the worldwide Flood.

Dr. Johnson concludes by stating: "Although the illustrations above only serve to introduce this fascinating trove of pictographic philology (word study), they do show what forensic professionals call a "beyond-genuine-dispute" witness of God's historic workings in Chinese history, producing a form of providential history and evidence of biblical truth."

China has multiple flood legends from numerous people groups in the country. Below are a few interesting ones that have strong connections to Genesis (compiled by Nick Liguori, author of *Echoes of Ararat*).

Han Flood Legends

The Han are the majority people group in China. They have a knowledge of the Deluge recorded in their ancient writings. It is no simple task to read and interpret ancient Chinese history. There is also much that we do not know, much still being debated by Chinese scholars, and there are texts inaccessible to us. I lean on the insights of others on this topic. The historian Sharon Turner wrote:[48]

"The Chinese literature has several notices of this awful catastrophe. The Chou-king [Shoo-King], the history of China written by Confucius, opens with a representation of their country **being still under the effect of the waters.** ... Yao, their most ancient sovereign, acknowledged by Confucius, is introduced abruptly as saying to his ministers, "**Alas! the deluging waters are spreading destruction. They surround the mountains. They overtop the hills. They rise high, and extend wide as the spacious vault of heaven.**"[49] The opposing school of the Tao-see also speak of **the Deluge as occurring under "Niu-hoa,"** whom they make a female. The seasons were then changed: day and night confounded: **great waters later overspread the universe, and men were reduced to the condition of fishes.**[50] Other Chinese writers refer to the same event. ... The celebrated Kong-in-ta adds, that **the waters overwhelmed the animals and all habitations.**[51] Tcha-che alludes to them, and Mong-tsee remarks, "Under Yao, the empire was not yet formed. **The stagnant waters of the Deluge still covered the plains,** and what was not under water was covered with trees."[52] By cutting large canals, Yao made the country habitable."[53]

One of the potential challenges with this account is that the Shoo-King or "Book of History" associates this devastating flood with the Yellow River. That being the case, we must ask whether this book is describing a global flood or a local one. James Legge (1815–1897), who himself translated the Shoo-King into English, addressed this issue in his introduction, saying that the Shoo-King seems to contain **an imperfect reference to the global Flood:**

> But now, according to the views which I have sought to establish, the labors of Yu are not history, but myth. He did not perform the prodigious achievements on the mountains and rivers which are ascribed to him. ... The labors of Yu being denied, no place is left in his time for the deluge of Yao. The

utmost that can be allowed is an inundation of the Ho [Yellow River], destructive enough, no doubt, but altogether unfit to be described in the words put into the mouths of Yao, Shun, and Yu about it. Did the compilers of the first Parts of the Shoo draw upon their fancy for the floods that embraced the mountains and overtopped the hills and assailed the heavens? **Or did they find them in the tradition of the deluge by which 'all the hills that were under the whole heaven were covered.'** I prefer to take the suggestion in the latter question as the fact, and therefore think that in the description of the inundation of Yao's time **we have an imperfect reference to the deluge of Noah.**[54]

A Chinese scholar named Yang Lihui noted that the Chinese have "historicized" or "edited" some of their ancient texts, to make them more rationally or philosophically palatable. This may be one reason for the imperfection of the Shoo-King's account of the Flood.

Miao (China)

The Miao are a people group inhabiting southwest China, composed of many subtribes with differing languages and customs. Their oral traditions are remarkably well-preserved, containing genealogies which appear to go back to Japheth. They have been noted by surrounding tribes for their lighter hair color and skin tone. Blonde, light brown, and red hair color have been observed among them, leading some historians to suggest they are of Indo-European origin, perhaps having migrated from Persia or Central Asia. Their use of songs in couplet form, to tell their genealogies and traditions, has helped them to be preserved quite accurately.[55]

One of the Miao tribes told this Flood tradition to a missionary named Edgar Truax, who labored among them from the 1920s to the 1940s.

> **So it poured 40 days in sheets and in torrents.** Then 55 days of misting and drizzle. **The waters surmounted the mountains and ranges. The deluge ascending** leapt valley and hollow. An earth

with **no earth upon which to take refuge!** A world
with no foothold where one might subsist! The
people were baffled, impotent and ruined,
Despairing, horror stricken, diminished and finished.
**But the Patriarch Nuah was righteous. The
Matriarch Gaw Bo-lu-en upright. Built a boat
very wide. Made a ship very vast. Their household
entire got aboard and were floated, the family
complete rode the deluge in safety. The animals
with him were female and male. The birds went
along and were mated in pairs.** When the time was
fulfilled, God commanded the waters. The day had
arrived, **the flood waters receded.**
Then Nuah liberated a dove from their refuge,
Sent a bird to go forth and bring again tidings.
The flood had gone down into lake and to ocean;
The mud was confined to the pools and the hollows.
There was land once again where a man might reside;
there was a place in the earth now to rear habitations.
Buffalo then were brought, **an oblation to God,**
Fatter cattle became sacrifice to the Mighty. **The
Divine One then gave them His blessing**; their God
then bestowed His good graces.[56]

They also have this tradition of the Tower of Babel, and their genealogy. Note the similarity to the Genesis names of Ham, Shem, Cush, Mizraim, Japheth, Elem, Asshur, and Gomer:

**Lo-han then begat Cusah and Mesay. Lo-shan
begat Elan and Nga-shur. Their offspring
begotten became tribes and peoples;** their
descendants established encampments and cities.
Their singing was all with the same tunes and music;
**their speaking was all with the same words and
language.** Then they said let us build us a very big
city; **let us raise unto heaven a very high tower.**
This was wrong, but they reached this decision; not
right, but they rashly persisted. **God struck at them
then, changed their language and accent.**
Descending in wrath, He confused tones and voices.

One's speech to the others who hear him has no meaning; he's speaking in words, but they can't understand him. So the city they built was never completed; the tower they wrought has to stand thus unfinished. In despair then they separate under all heaven, **they part from each other the globe to encircle.** They arrive at six corners and speak the six languages. ... **The Patriarch Jahphu** got the center of nations. The son he begat was **the Patriarch Gomen.** Who took him a wife called the Matriarch Goyong. Their grandson and his wife both took the name Tutan. Their descendants are given in order as follows: Patriarch Gawndan Mew-wan, Matriarch Cawdan Mew-jew; Patriarch Jenku Dawvu, Matriarch Jeneo Boje; Patriarch Gangen Newang (wife not given); Patriarch Seageweng, Matriarch Maw gueh. Their children, eleven in number, was each the head of a family. Five branches became the Miao nation. Six families joined with the Chinese."[57]

Their tradition of Creation also seems to refer to Genesis themes:

On the day God created the heavens and earth.
On that day He opened the gateway of light.
In the earth then He made heaps of earth and of stone.
In the sky He made bodies, the sun and the moon.
In the earth He created the hawk and the kite.
In the water created the lobster and fish.
In the wilderness made He the tiger and bear,
Made verdure to cover the mountains,
Made forest extend with the ranges,
Made the light green cane,
Made the rank bamboo.

...On the earth He created a man from the dirt.
Of the man thus created, a woman He formed.
Then the Patriarch Dirt made a balance of stones.
Estimated the weight of the earth to the bottom.
Calculated the bulk of the heavenly bodies.

And pondered the ways of the Deity, God.
The Patriarch Dirt begat Patriarch Se-teh.
The Patriarch Se-Teh begat a son Lusu.
And Lusu had Gehlo and he begat Lama.
The Patriarch Lama begat the man Nuah.
His wife was the Matriarch Gaw Bo-lu-en.
Their sons were Lo Han, Lo Shen and Jah-hu.
So the earth began filling with tribes and with families.
Creation was shared by the clans and the peoples.[58]

This remarkable account is also attested by the early missionary Samuel Clarke (1854–1946), who labored for over 30 years in the Guizhou province:

> The Miao of that region [Guizhou Province] say that **the land was all divided among the three sons of Noah, who were the ancestors of the Miao, Chinese, and No-su.** The Miao are the descendants of the eldest son. Unfortunately when the land was divided, they only used straw ropes for boundaries, while the Nosu used stones. A fire occurred which burnt up their boundary ropes, but left the No-su stones uninjured. Thus they lost their land![59]

Maori (China)

The Maori priests meticulously guarded their ancient historical traditions. Around the 1860s, they shared with one John White a stunning tradition of the Flood, matching the Genesis account in several details. They told that God sent the Flood because "evil prevailed everywhere," and that two righteous people "built a house on the raft, and put much food into it." After the Flood, which drowned everyone except those saved on the giant raft, the survivors got off and offered a sacrifice to God, and "then looking up, they beheld the rainbow."[60]

How It All Happened: Catastrophic Plate Tectonics

Natural history museums have displays and animations that try to make the case that the continents were once joined in a formation called Pangea and then slowly moved apart to their current locations over tens of millions of years. Well, it's actually quite obvious that the continents were in fact together at one time—evolutionists and most creationists agree on this point. But did they really spread apart slowly over millions of years, or did it happen rapidly—even within just one year—during the Flood of Noah's time? This chapter explains how.

The conventional idea presented in museums is that Pangea began breaking apart about 175 million years ago and the continents have been moving apart slowly to their current locations.[61] Today we can use GPS measurements to confirm the direction and speed of their movement, which is in fact just inches per year. But has it always been this way, with the continents moving apart slowly? Actually, it hasn't, and we'll explain why this is the case, both biblically and scientifically.

The Bible records that the Flood commenced by the "fountains of the great deep" *breaking open*. The Hebrew term used for this is bâqa' (pronounced "baw-kah") which means to "cleave, rend, or break and rip open; to make a breach." This "cleaving and breaking/ripping open" couldn't describe what we see on the planet today any better.

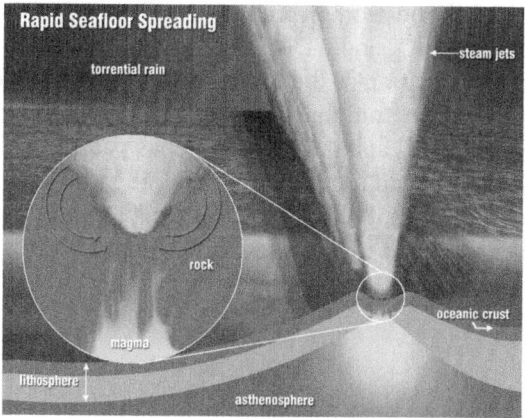

Figure 9. Fountains of the Great Deep Breaking Open (the Beginning of Noah's Flood).[62]

In 1994 six PhD scientists published a research paper titled, "Catastrophic Plate Tectonics: A Global Flood Model of Earth History,"[63] that substantiated this biblical aspect of the Flood. Their research revealed that fast-moving, subducting oceanic plates were responsible for the continents breaking apart and spreading to their current locations, in contrast to the evolutionary ideas of slow continental drift and equally slow seafloor spreading. Ongoing research in this area has shown that the model helps explain volcanoes, mountain ranges, the shapes and positions of continents, and the generation of global tsunamis that explain some rock layers.

Genesis Apologetics worked with many of these leading Flood geologists to produce YouTube videos that visualize how CPT played such a large role in Noah's Flood.[64] Readers interested in a more technical explanation behind the catastrophic nature of the Flood are encouraged to view Dr. Steve Austin's presentation titled, "Continental Sprint: A Global Flood Model for Earth History."[65]

Much of the fundamental research on the topic of CPT has been undertaken by Dr. John Baumgardner over the past 40 years. As a professional scientist, Dr. Baumgardner is known for developing TERRA, a finite element code designed to study flow of rock within the Earth's mantle. In 1997, *US News and World Report* described him as "the world's pre-eminent expert in the design of computer models for geophysical convection."[66] Baumgardner has applied TERRA to demonstrate that the Earth's mantle is indeed vulnerable to runaway instability and that this instability is capable of resurfacing the planet in the time span of just a few months. We'll review many of Baumgardner's findings below.

Brief Summary of Plate Tectonics Concepts

Scientists of both creation and evolutionary persuasions agree that new ocean crust forms at ocean rift zones where two tectonic plates are moving apart. The plates in the rift migrate apart, magma rises to fill the gap, is cooled by ocean water, and solidifies to make a strip of new ocean crust. The two plates are each like a conveyor belt that moves away from the rift zone along one edge and usually toward a subduction zone along the other edge. At the subduction zone, the moving plate plunges into the mantle beneath and thus disappears from the surface (see Figure 10).

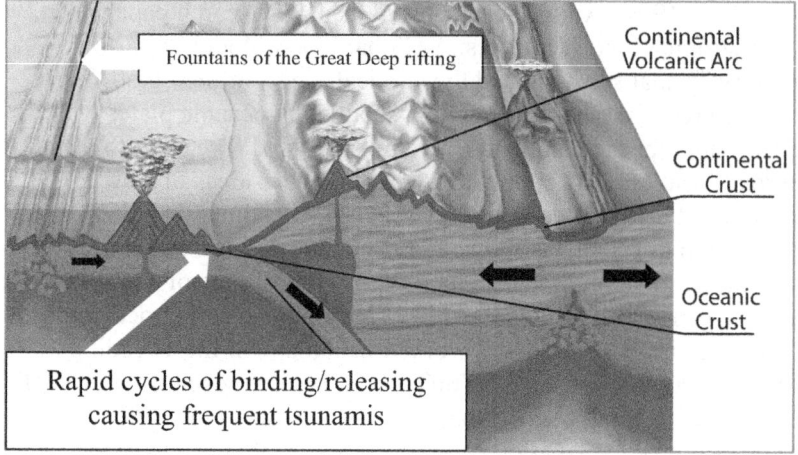

Figure 10. Subduction Overview.

The main difference between the creationist and secular understanding is that, in the creationist understanding, during the Flood, plate speeds were about five miles-per-hour instead of just a few inches per year, as they are measured to be today. The much higher speed is why the process during the Flood is referred to as *Catastrophic* Plate Tectonics (CPT).[67]

What evidence is there for plate tectonics?

The evidence supporting the concept of plate tectonics is overwhelming. Let's quickly tour some of the key evidences, starting first with the "big picture," then investigating some of the physical evidences in more detail.

Evidence 1: The continents fit together like puzzle pieces

One of the clearest evidences is that the continents fit together like puzzle pieces. While many school textbooks credit Alfred Wegener, a meteorologist, with the "discovery" that the continents "drifted" from an original super-continent (Pangea or similar configuration) to their current location, it was actually a creation scientist who brought this to light much earlier. His name was Antonio Snider-Pellegrini (1802–1885), a French geographer and scientist, who theorized about the possibility of continental drift. In

1858, Snider-Pellegrini published his book, La Création et ses mystères dévoilés ("The Creation and its Mysteries Unveiled") which included the image in Figure 11.

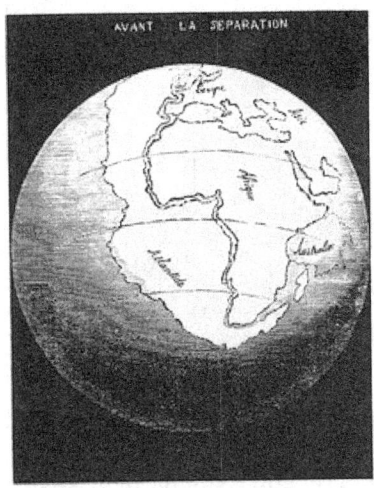
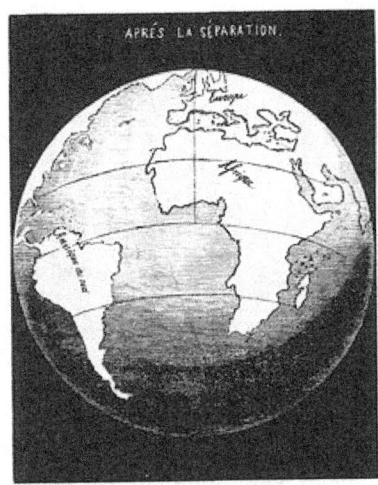

Figure 11. Snider-Pellegrini made these two maps in 1858, showing his interpretation of how the American and African continents once fit together before becoming separated.

Snider-Pellegrini based his theory on the Genesis Flood, the obvious shape and fitting of the continents, and the fact that plant fossils found in both Europe and the United States were identical.[68]

Modern mapping technologies and the help of bathymetric maps that reveal the shapes and contours of the continental shelf and the ocean floor allow us to clearly see that the continents were once connected and later torn apart. Figure 12 shows what Earth looks like with all the ocean water removed. Without the oceans, the deep shelves on each side of the continents become visible and we can see how the continents fit together like puzzle pieces to shape an Earth that used to be mostly a single land mass.

Interestingly, this perfectly fits the Genesis account: "Then God said, 'Let the waters under the heavens be gathered together into one place, and let the dry land appear'; and it was so. And God called the dry land Earth, and the gathering together of the waters He called Seas. And God saw that it was good" (Genesis 1:9–10). This is especially obvious when looking at the matching jagged edges of lower South America and Africa (see Figure 13).

43

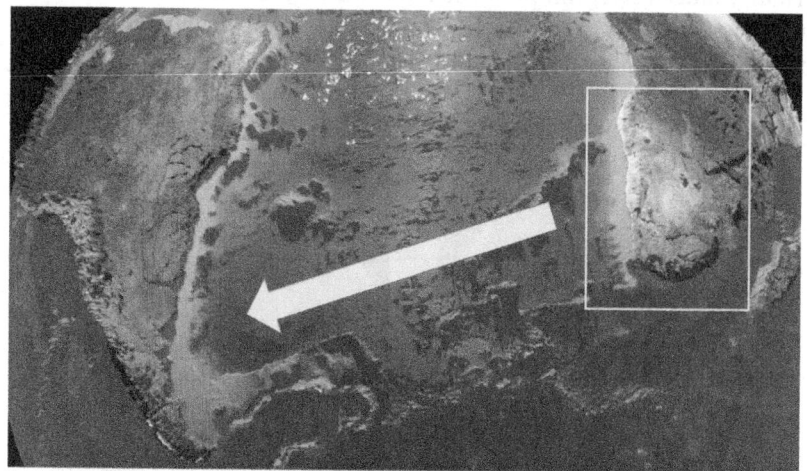

Figure 12. Lower South America Matching Africa.[69]

We can also see how a notch of submerged land off the grand banks of Newfoundland fits nearly perfectly into a slot north of Spain (see Figure 13).

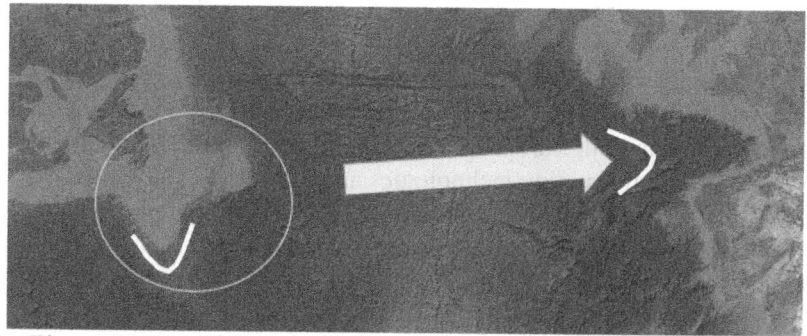

Figure 13. Submerged land off the Grand Banks of Newfoundland fitting into a Slot North of Spain (Google Earth).

From a Biblical standpoint, the continents fit together so well because of the catastrophic linear rifting that occurred when the fountains of the great deep were "cleaved" and pulled apart only a few thousand years ago.

Evidence 2: The Oceanic Ridge System

The oceanic ridge system covers more than 40,000 miles and circles the Earth 1.6 times over.

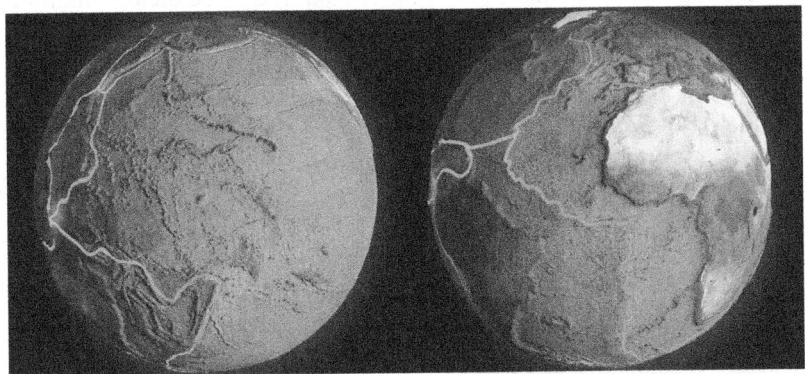

Figure 14. Oceanic Ridge System.

The Mid-Atlantic Ridge (MAR) represents one of the largest rifts left behind by the global seafloor spreading process. It looks like a giant baseball seam running around the face of the Earth.

Figure 15. Mid-Atlantic Ridge (MAR).[70]

The MAR is part of the longest mountain range in the world and includes perpendicular faults along its entire length, known as transform faults, showing the formation of new seafloor involved a pulling apart of the ocean basin. The sharpness of the faults and the abrupt edges indicate that little time has expired since their formation. The raised and sloped features on each side of the rift also testify to the hot and buoyant rock that still lies beneath it. From a Biblical standpoint, the formation of the Atlantic basin occurred quickly during the Flood and then slowed down greatly to about an inch per year, as GPS measurements today indicate.

Evidence 3: Ring of Fire

The Ring of Fire is a 25,000-mile horseshoe-shaped string of oceanic trenches in the Pacific Ocean basin where about 90% of the world's earthquakes and a large fraction of the world's volcanoes occur.[71] It is also where most of the plate subduction is taking place today. From a Biblical perspective, this long belt of volcanoes and earthquakes marks the location where vast amounts of ocean plate was rapidly subducted into the Earth's interior during the Flood. Today, by comparison, the speed of subduction is extremely slow, and the resulting earthquakes and tsunamis are dramatically less frequent.

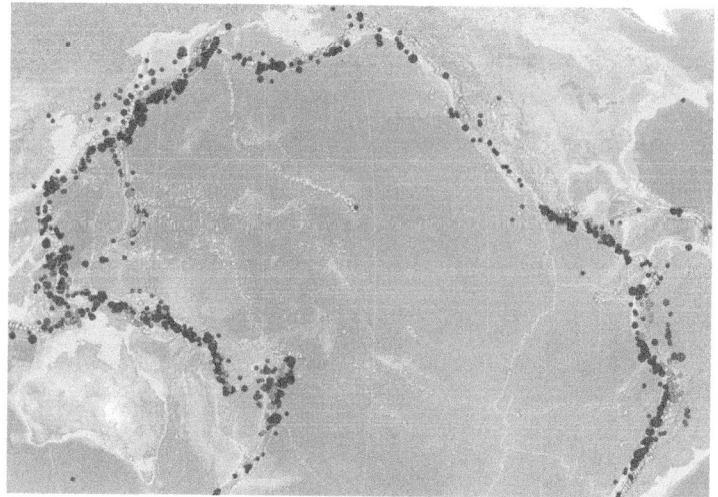

Figure 16. USGS 1900–2013 Earthquakes in the Ring of Fire.[72]

How is CPT different from the secular understanding of plate tectonics?

CPT is basically the expression at the Earth's surface of a recent, massive, and rapid overturn of rock inside the region inside the Earth known as the mantle, which is the 1,800-mile thick layer of rock between the Earth's core and its crust. Regions of cooler rock in the upper part of the mantle have a natural tendency to sink downward toward the bottom, and regions of warmer rock at the bottom have a natural tendency to rise upward toward the surface. When conditions are right, this natural tendency for rising and sinking can "run away," such that both rising and sinking become faster and faster—up to a billion times faster. The force responsible for driving this behavior is simply gravity. From a Biblical perspective, the runaway episode responsible for CPT occurred during the Flood described in Genesis 6–8.

The possibility that runaway behavior might occur in the mantle was discovered decades ago in laboratory studies[73] that explored how mantle minerals deform at mantle temperature and stress conditions. These basic experiments revealed that mantle minerals weaken by factors of more than a billion for stress levels that can readily arise inside the Earth. Computer experiments[74] later confirmed that episodes of runaway overturn in the mantle are inevitable under the right conditions because of this inherent weakening behavior demonstrated in these laboratory experiments.

What might be the consequences at the Earth's surface of a runaway overturn event in the mantle? One notable consequence is that the tectonic plates at the Earth's surface get caught up in the rapid flow of rock within the mantle beneath. In particular, the ocean plates diving into the mantle at the deep-ocean trenches during the overturn did so at a spectacularly accelerated pace compared to today's rates. Likewise, in zones known today as spreading ridges (such as the Mid-Atlantic Ridge) where tectonic plates are moving apart from one another, the speed of separation during the overturn was dramatically higher.

Just how much faster would the plate motions during such an overturn event be compared with what is occurring today? This can be estimated based on the time frame provided in the Bible's account of the Flood and on the amount of plate motion associated with the part of the rock record that contains fossils of the plants and animals buried in the Flood. From these numbers one obtains a plate speed on the order of five miles-per-hour. A typical plate speed today, as measured by GPS, is on the order of a couple inches per year. The ratio of these two speeds is about one billion to one.

What are other noteworthy consequences of such rapid plate motions? One is that water on the ocean bottom in the zones where plates were moving apart so rapidly was in direct contact with the molten rock which was rising from below to fill the gap between the plates. This molten rock at about 1300° C converted the ocean water to steam at extremely high pressure. This steam organized to form in a linear chain of intense supersonic jets along the entire midocean ridge system. As these jets pierced the layer of ocean water above where they were formed, they entrained massive amounts of liquid seawater, which was lofted high above the Earth. This liquid water then fell back to the surface as rain. Hence, a direct consequence of rapid plate motions was persisting rain over much if not most of the Earth.

A second prominent consequence of rapid plate motion was a rising sea level that flooded the land surface with ocean water. The rising sea level resulted from a decrease in the volume of the ocean basins. Behind that decrease was the loss of original cold ocean plate as it plunged into the mantle at an ocean trench and its replacement with new and much warmer ocean plate produced by seafloor spreading at a mid-ocean ridge. The new plate was on average 500–1000° C warmer than the cold plate it replaced. Because warm rock of a given mass has more volume than cold rock of the same mass, the ocean floor above new ocean floor was 0.6–1.2 miles higher than was the old ocean floor. As more and more new ocean floor was generated at mid-ocean ridges, while more and more of the original ocean floor was removed by recycling into the mantle, the global sea level relative to the land surface rose by thousands of feet. Hence, a notable result of rapid plate motion was a rising sea level and a dramatic flooding of the continents by ocean water.

A third major consequence of the rapid plate motion is the generation of a huge number of giant tsunamis. In today's world, at an ocean trench where an oceanic plate is steadily slipping into the mantle, the adjacent overriding plate generally is locked against it and is bent downward as the other plate slides into the mantle (see Figure

17). As this motion proceeds, the overriding plate is deformed more and more in a spring-like manner until a stress limit is exceeded. At this point the two plates unlock, significant slip between the plates occurs, and the overriding plate returns to its original shape. Such an unlocking and slip event usually produces an earthquake. If the slip event is large enough it also can launch a tsunami. During the Flood, when plate speeds were a billion times faster than today, it is almost certain that this same locking and unlocking phenomenon also prevailed. The higher plate speeds and the huge amount of seafloor recycled into the mantle would have generated vast numbers of huge tsunamis. Conservative estimates are in the range of 50,000–100,000 or more tsunamis, with wave heights in the range of hundreds of feet or higher.

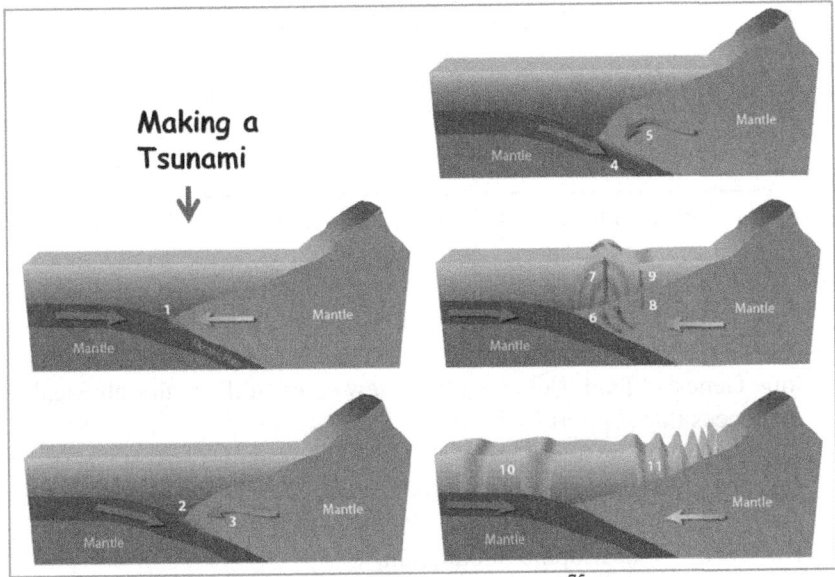

Figure 17. Making a Tsunami.[75]

Numerical experiments undertaken by Dr. Baumgardner to model the erosion and sediment deposition aspects of this sort of tsunami activity show that it is readily capable of producing the observed continent sediment record. This work is described in a recent paper titled, "Understanding how the Flood sediment record was formed: The role of large tsunamis."[76] Figure 18 shows a plot from this simulation that includes the plate motions.[77] Hence, a third major result of rapid plate motion is the formation of the observed layer-cake pattern of fossil-bearing sediments across the continents.

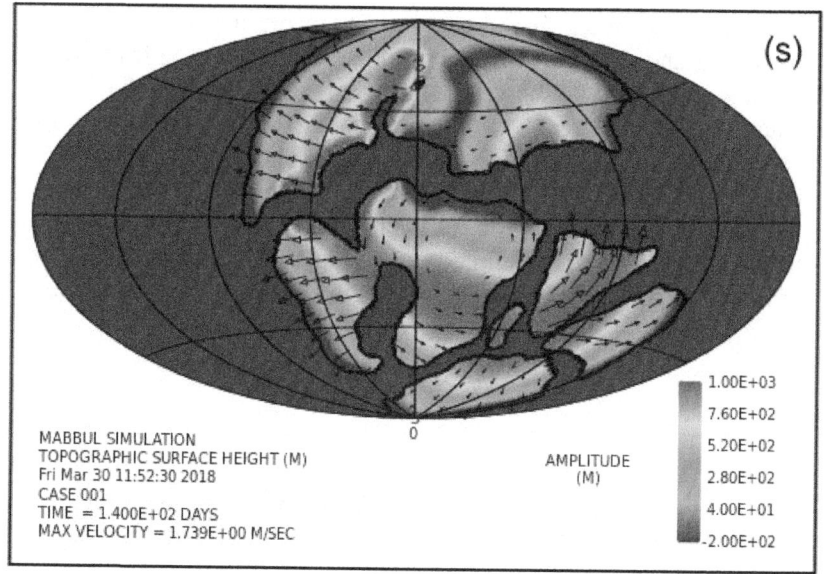

Figure 18. Plot from Dr. John Baumgardner's CPT Tsunami Simulation.[78]

Dr. Baumgardner's simulation allows us in a limited way to rewind time to gain some insight into what happened during the year-long Genesis Flood. Below we'll review some of the major physical evidences that support CPT.

Physical evidences that support the reality of CPT

Evidence 1: Catastrophic Subduction

The oceanic plates that rapidly subducted under the continents during the Flood are still visible! Seismic images of the mantle reveal a ring of unexpectedly cold rock at the bottom of the mantle, beneath the subduction zones that surround the Pacific Ocean. We say *unexpectedly* cold rock because if a slab of crust subducts very slowly, it will develop thermal equilibrium with the surrounding mantle rocks as it sinks. The temperature will even out. However, evening out the temperature takes a lot of time. If the slab subducts slowly, at the rate it moves today, there is plenty of time for heat to transfer and make the subducting slab match the temperature of the surrounding mantle. If the slab subducts rapidly, there is no time for the heat to transfer and the subducted slab stays cooler than the surrounding rocks for thousands of years. Thus, the temperature difference we observe strongly suggests rapid subduction, much faster than is occurring today.

This structure is obtained using a technique known as seismic tomography that folds together data from 10,000 or more seismograms at once (see Figure 19).

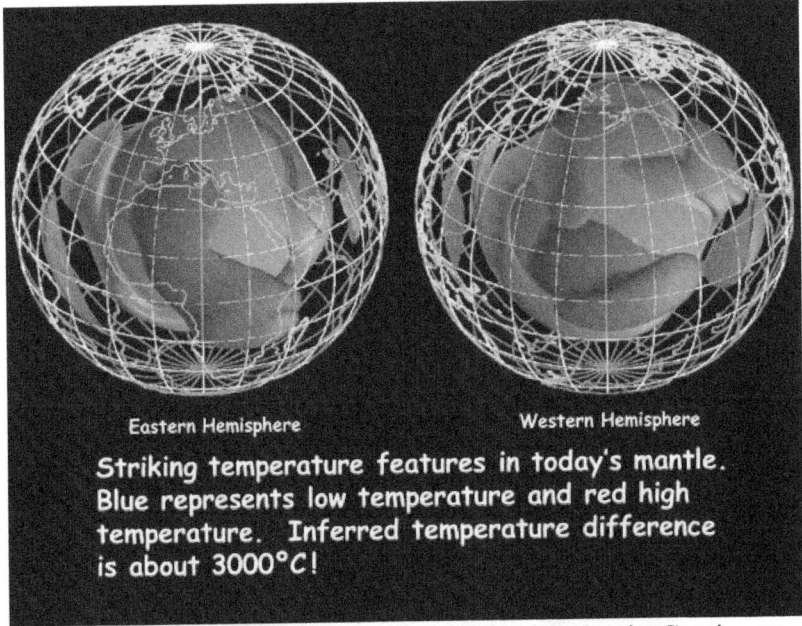

Figure 19. Cold Plates (Blue) that Subducted under the Continents During the Flood.[79]

Evidence 2: The Fossil Record

The action of CPT caused the oceanic plates to subduct rapidly under the land masses and generate cycles of tsunamis that brought staggering quantities of sediment onto land that wiped out every living creature in their paths, burying them in the mud layers we still see today. These types of tsunamis still occur, although much less frequently and on a smaller scale. The moving sea floor subducts, snags under the land masses, and then releases, creating mud-filled tsunamis that carry debris and sea life onto land, sorting them in layers.

Giant, high-frequency tsunamis that were occurring during the Flood explain why today we see dinosaur graveyards around the world, including 13 states in the middle of America, containing dead dinosaurs mixed with marine life (see Figure 20). What type of flood could do this? Just how much water would it take to bury millions of land creatures under hundreds of feet of mud and sand in the Morrison Formation (a 13-state, 700,000 square mile area)?

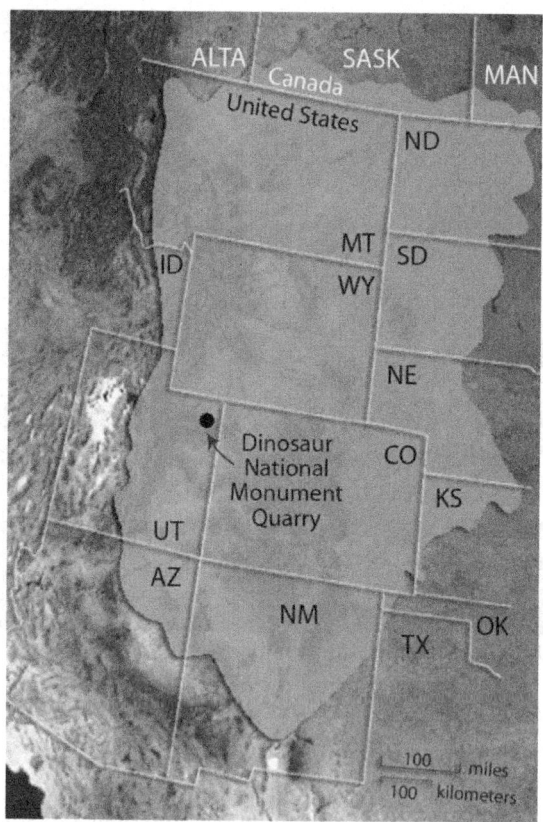

Figure 20. Morrison Formation.[80]

Just how did so many land creatures get buried together with marine life, with 97% of the dinosaurs found disarticulated,[81] and many of the remaining 3% that are found intact discovered in mud and sand layers with their necks arched back, suffocating as they died?[82]

A global inundation that covered most of North America is no secret to secular geologists, but they call it something different: the "widespread Late Cretaceous transgression"[83] (essentially technical jargon for "worldwide flood"). Studies have revealed that "a sea level rise of 310 meters is required to flood the Cretaceous layers based on their current elevation." The challenge for secular geologists, however, is that the maximum thickness of the fossil layers produced by a 310-meter sea level rise is only about 700 meters, but in North America, nearly 50 percent of the Cretaceous layers contain strata *thicker* than 700 meters.

Sediment transport via highly turbulent tsunami-driven flow described in Baumgardner's published work logically seems to be required to account for these thick layers. These layers also suggest that the continents had to *down warp* locally during this global inundation, as Baumgardner's modeling likewise suggests. This is what CPT predicts and what the Flood would have done. There's just no way that rising sea levels alone can explain the fossil record in North America—mechanisms much more powerful and catastrophic *had to be involved.*

Evidence 3: Fossil Correlation[84]

By comparing fossils of small organisms found on the ocean floor with fossils of the same organisms on different continents, it has been possible to determine when the ocean crust formed in terms of the fossil sequence found in the continental sediments. What has been discovered, both from a creationist as well as from a secular understanding, is that much of the continental fossil record was already in place before any of the present-day ocean crust had come into existence. For example, all the trilobite fossils had already been deposited, plus all the older coal deposits (Pennsylvanian System coals) had already been formed before any of the present-day ocean crust had formed.

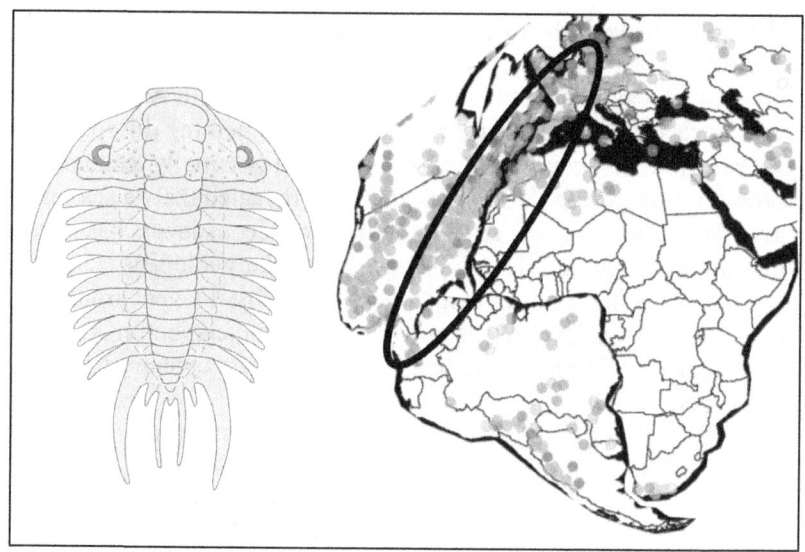

Figure 21. Reassembling the continents shows a trilobite habitat torn apart by the Flood.[85]

The fossil record (e.g., certain trilobite species) that now straddles both sides of the MAR testify to the rapid nature of this catastrophe, with millions of the same kinds of animals that were once living together now found buried in mud and lime layers on either side of the rift.

In the creationist understanding, the presence of fossils is a trustworthy indicator of the action of the Flood, meaning that a large part of the Flood cataclysm had already unfolded and had generated fossil-bearing sediments on the continental surface *before* any of the present-day ocean floor had appeared. It further implies that all of today's ocean floor formed *since the onset of the Flood*, during roughly the latter half of the cataclysm. It also means that all the pre-Flood ocean floor, plus any ocean floor formed during the earlier portion of the Flood, must have been recycled into the Earth's interior during the cataclysm. These considerations indicate in a compelling way that rapid plate tectonics must have been a major aspect of the year-long Flood catastrophe.

Evidence 4: Buckled/Folded Sedimentary Layers

The Genesis Flood laid down tens of millions of cubic miles of sediment like sand and mud all over the globe. It soon hardened into rock. These layers contain most of the fossil record. Some of these massive layers are bent and even folded, proving they were laid down rapidly and then bent before hardening into rock. Otherwise they would have crumbled instead of bending plastically. These folded and bent geological features are found all over the world and most occurred during the latter stages of the Flood when 80% of the world's mountains rapidly formed.

Figure 22. Example of Massive Geologic Folding.[86]

Evidence 5: River Fans

If the evolutionary view about the continents were true (that they moved apart slowly over millions of years), the large rivers on the continents that empty into the Atlantic Ocean would have left a connected trail of mud stretching from one side of the Atlantic to the other. But what the evidence actually shows is that most of the seafloor spreading that formed the Atlantic was *over* before continental runoff and major transport of sediment into the Atlantic basin *began*. Major rivers like the Congo, Mississippi, and Amazon run off the continents and have mud fans with only thousands of years' worth of mud deposits—not millions.[87]

55

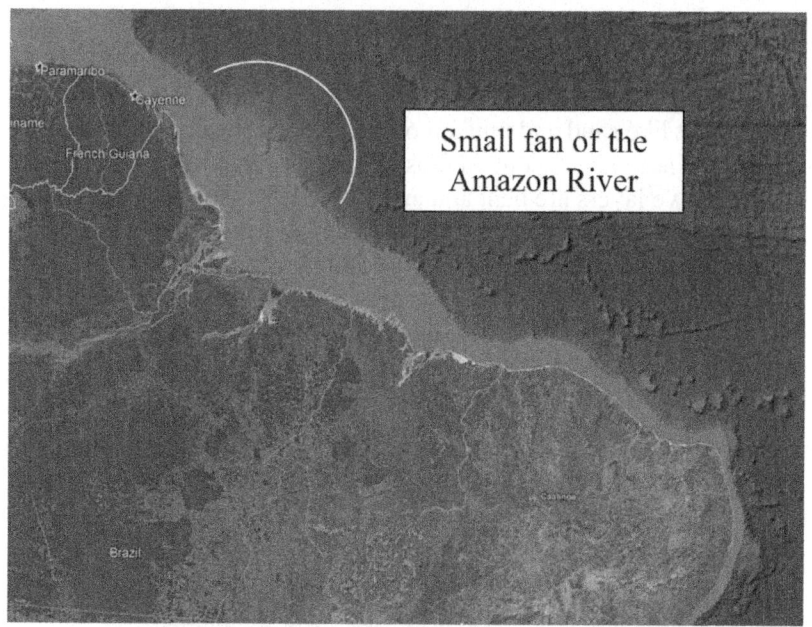

Figure 23. Amazon River Fan (Google Earth).

There are flat sand bottoms on each side of the continents showing they were split apart rapidly—they don't have millions of years' worth of runoff with considerable mud extending into the ocean. The continental shelves exhibit little erosion and still match nearly perfectly when put back together. Millions of years of erosion would have destroyed much of the sharp continental shelfs. These rivers began shaping and eroding only thousands of years ago, not millions.

Evidence 6: Sloss Megasequences

Dr. Tim Clarey has conducted extensive research on the Genesis Flood using over 2,000 stratigraphic columns (bore holes) from across North and South America, Africa, and Europe.[88] These data confirm the existence of six megasequences (called "Sloss-type megasequences"), large-scale sequences of sedimentary deposits that reveal six different stages of global depositions that occurred during the Flood.

The three earliest megasequences (Sauk, Tippecanoe, and Kaskaskia) contained mostly marine fossils, indicating that only shallow marine areas were swamped and buried by CPT-caused tsunamis. The 4th megasequence (Absaroka) shows a dramatic rise in ocean level and overall global coverage and volume. This sequence also includes the first major plant (coal) and terrestrial animal fossils. The 5th megasequence (Zuni) was mostly responsible for the demise of the dinosaurs and appears to be the highest water point of the Flood (its zenith) because it shows the highest levels of sediment coverage and volume compared to earlier megasequences. The final megasequence (Tejas) contains fossils from the highest upland areas of the pre-Flood world. Together, these megasequences explain why over 75% of Earth is covered by an average of about one mile of sedimentary deposits.

Figure 24. World Sediment Map (showing 75% of Earth's surface is covered by an average of about one mile of sedimentary deposits).

Evidence 7: Massive Coal Deposits

One of the highest and most severe stages of the Flood occurred during the 4th Sloss megasequence, the Absaroka. Land creatures and plants start showing up in the fossil record laid down by this megasequence. This is also the time when the world's ocean floor began to be created anew. In other words, the oldest ocean crust today only goes back to the time of the deposition of the Absaroka megasequence.

Notice the top bars in the first seven labeled rows in Figure 25. This shows the global animal fossil occurrences from the Paleobiology Database.[89] The lower, blue bars in each row represent aquatic animals and the top, red bars represent land animals. The megasequences are shown on the left. Note that few land animals appear until the end of the Kaskaskia, then land animals begin increasingly showing up in the fossil record as the Flood progressed.

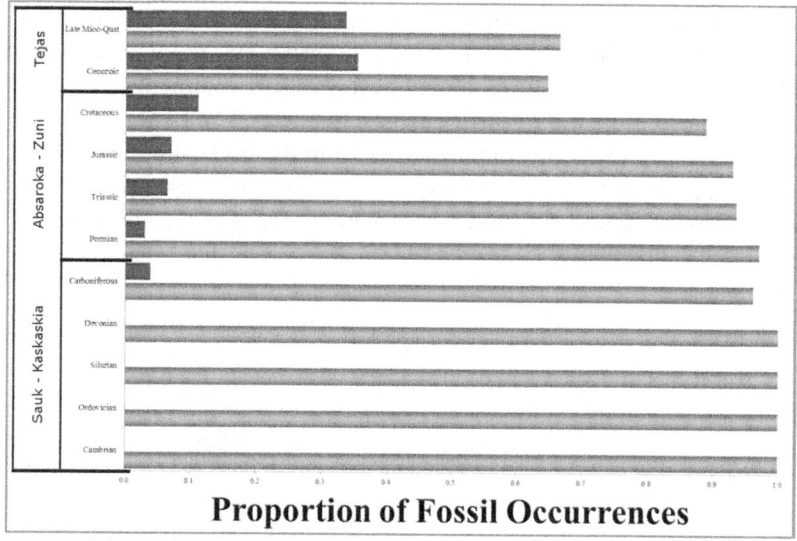

Figure 25. Sloss Megasequences and Fossil Deposits.[90]

Entire ecosystems were buried during this megasequence in enormous deposits that later turned into coal, such as the extensive Appalachian coal beds. Even more coal was formed in the later Zuni and Tejas Megasequences as the waters of the Flood rose yet higher. The U.S. has over seven trillion tons of coal reserves. Where did it all come from? While we know that coal is formed by dead plant material being sandwiched between sediment layers, we only have enough vegetation on the Earth's surface today to produce just a fraction of the existing coal reserves.[91] This shows that the pre-Flood world was mostly covered by lush vegetation. The rising Flood waters and tsunamis that were necessary to sweep over the land and bury vast amounts of vegetation that turned into coal are best explained by a catastrophe of worldwide proportions.

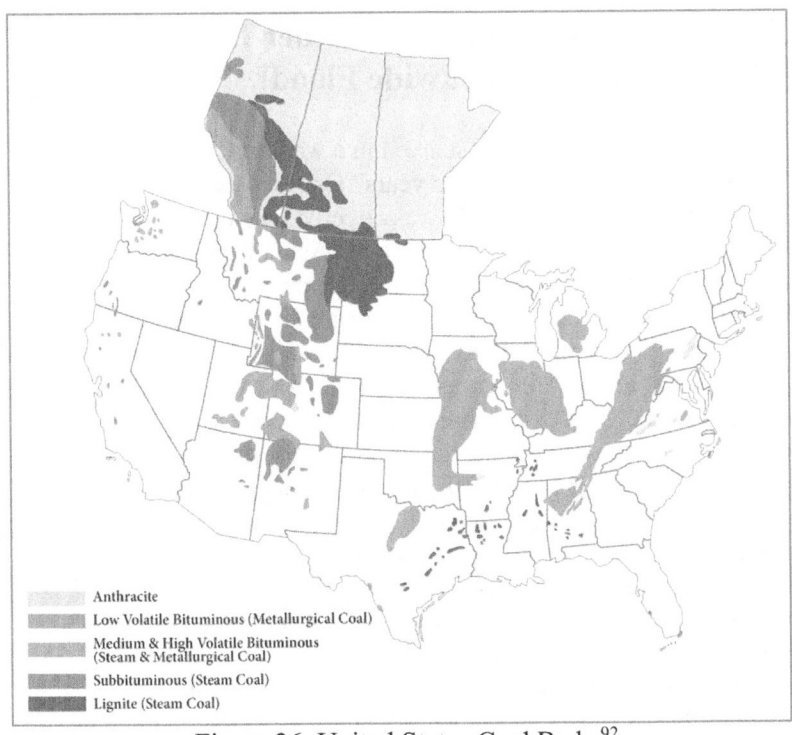

Figure 26. United States Coal Beds.[92]

In the later run-off stages of the Flood (called the Tejas sequence), plants swept off the pre-Flood lands formed massive coal beds such as in the Powder River Basin of Wyoming and Montana. The Powder River Basin layers are the largest coal deposits in North America, currently supplying over 40% of the coal in the U.S. Some of these stacked coal beds are up to 200 feet thick and cover areas that are 60 miles long by 60 miles wide. The sheer volume of plant material required to form such a massive layer of coal testifies to catastrophic circumstances.

Dinosaur Fossils: Look No Further If You Want Evidence for the Worldwide Flood!

Are the fossils really stacked in a way that proves life evolved on Earth over millions of unseen years? Or, does the fossil record provide evidence that the world was covered by a massive Flood in Noah's time just thousands of years ago? Actually, the fossil record does not show increasingly complex life emerging over the millennia. What it shows is a record of death in the order that the creatures were buried during the worldwide flood.

Think about it for a minute—Genesis 7 verse 11 says that the fountains of the great deep were broken up and the windows of heaven were opened, creating floods and tidal waves that were unimaginable. The Bible says the flood waters increased upon the Earth for 150 days until all the high hills under heaven were covered with over 20 feet of water. This process successively buried all creatures outside the Ark based on where they lived as the Flood waters prevailed, how smart they were, their means and speed of mobility, and their body density. This is precisely why the fossil record generally shows the shallow-water marine creatures buried in the lower layers. Then, as the ocean waters rose higher and higher the suffocated fish were buried, followed by amphibians, reptiles, mammals, and then birds.

President of Answers in Genesis, Ken Ham, has become well-known for making this statement: "If there really was a Global Flood, what would the evidence be? Billions of dead things, buried in rock layers, laid down by water all over the Earth." This is exactly what we see.

For example, the Paleobiology Database is a free, searchable database that is designed to "provide global, collection-based occurrence and taxonomic data for organisms of all geological ages."[93] This database includes 183,739 fossil *collections* totaling 1,323,009 *occurrences* (with each "occurrence" ranging from a few fossils to numerous). From a Biblical Creation standpoint, the Genesis Flood deposited the vast majority of these fossils, and the chapters that follow explain the mechanics behind how it happened. Each of the circle dots in Figure 27 shows the extent of the known fossil record.

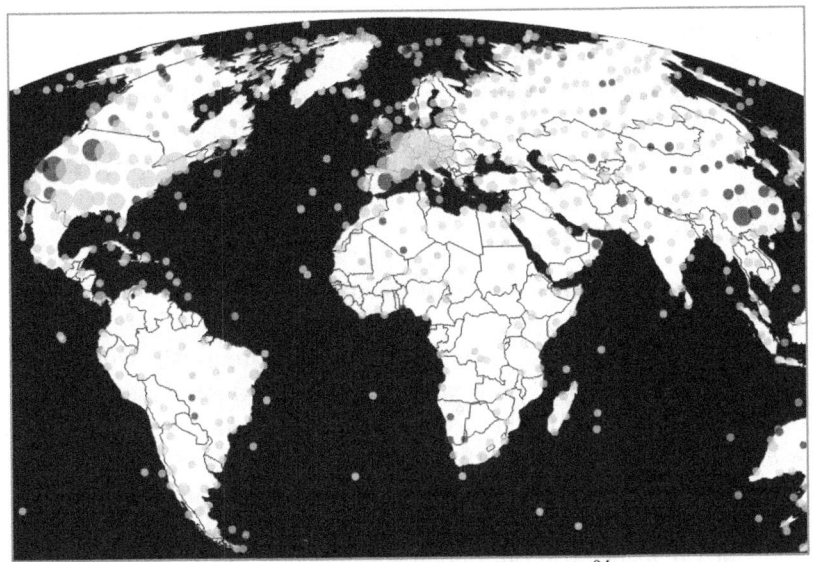

Figure 27. Paleobiology Database.[94]

If the untestable assumptions that hold up the ideas of radiometric dating are not true (and we believe they are not[95]), then Figure 27 displays a massive, watery graveyard, most of which was filled during the year-long Genesis Flood.

Even Charles Darwin said, "… as by evolution theory, innumerable transitional forms must have existed, why do we not find them embedded in countless numbers in the crust of the Earth?" and "Why is not every geological formation and every stratum full of such intermediate links? Geology assuredly does not reveal any such finely graduated organic chain; and this is the most obvious and serious objection which can be urged against the theory?" Darwin expected that these challenges would be resolved after more research was conducted. But today, 150 years and millions of fossils later, the proof **still** doesn't exist.

When the famous Dr. Colin Patterson of the British Museum of Natural History was asked why evolutionary transitions were not included in his book titled, "Evolution" Patterson said: "I fully agree with your comments on the lack of direct illustration of evolutionary transitions in my book. If I knew of any, fossil or living, I would certainly have included them… You say that I should at least show a photo of the fossil from which each type organism was derived.' I will lay it on the line—there is not one such fossil for which one could make a watertight argument." Wow—after working with thousands of fossils for over 16 years in one of the largest natural history museums in the world, he makes a statement like this!

With this "big picture" overview provided, next we'll look into the dinosaur fossil record specifically, as well as a few of the leading supposed "transitional" fossils that are often displayed in museums to promote evolution.

Overview of the Dinosaur Fossil Record

The number of dinosaur "mass graves" around the world is astounding. These fossil graveyards contain a mixture of many different kinds of fossils that were *transported by large volumes of water* (see Figure 28). Modern, small-scale debris flows offer examples of what likely entrained, in some cases, millions of animals. Like a giant water wing, a debris flow carries its load largely undisturbed inside, as it rides upon a watery cushion either underwater or over land. As soon as the flow slows to a certain speed, turbulence overwhelms the load and it drops in place.

Figure 28. Dinosaur Fossil Graveyard Example.

Bone fossils typically occur as broken fragments. They were violently carried along with enormous amounts of mud and shifting sediments. By studying some of these fossil graveyards, we can gather clues that will demonstrate that the Flood was in fact catastrophic and worldwide, as stated in Genesis 7:20–23:

The waters rose and covered the mountains to a depth of more than fifteen cubits [at least 22 feet]. *Every living thing* that moved on land perished—birds, livestock, wild animals, *all the creatures* that swarm over the Earth, and *all mankind*. Everything on dry land that had the breath of life in its nostrils died. *Every living thing* on the face of the earth was wiped out; people and animals and the creatures that move along the ground and the birds were wiped from the Earth. *Only Noah was left*, and those with him in the ark. (emphasis added)

If this passage in Genesis is true, we would expect to find *billions of dead things buried in rock layers laid down by water all over the Earth.*[96] This is exactly what we find *all over the world*, and dinosaurs fossils are an incredibly good example of this.

A profound example of a dinosaur graveyard is Dinosaur National Monument in Utah, which is only a part of the 700,000-square mile Morrison Formation, a geologic unit that has spawned excavations of more than a hundred dinosaur quarries.[97]

Figure 45. Aerial extent of the Morrison Formation.

What type of catastrophe could possibly bury hundreds of massive bone beds in this 700,000-square mile area? This region could quite possibly represent an enormous, ancient debris flow that only a worldwide watery catastrophe could explain. When it comes to looking at the burial conditions of dinosaurs that were wiped out in the Flood, only about 3,000 of the dinosaur fossils are found in "articulated"[98] condition (with most of the bones still in place). Because fossils representing over 100,000 dinosaurs have been found, this represents only about 3% of the dinosaur fossil record.[99] So these

63

animals did not die peacefully. Whatever wiped them out was *sudden* and *violent*.

Another characteristic about dinosaur bonebeds is the evidence that they were quickly buried in **mud**. The very fact that we have so many preserved dinosaur fossils shows that they were buried quickly because fossilization requires rapid burial in **muddy ground**. The fossil record is full of dinosaurs that suddenly died in watery graves around the world, with many of them found in the famous "death pose" with their necks arched back, as if drowning in mud and carried along by a mudflow.[100]

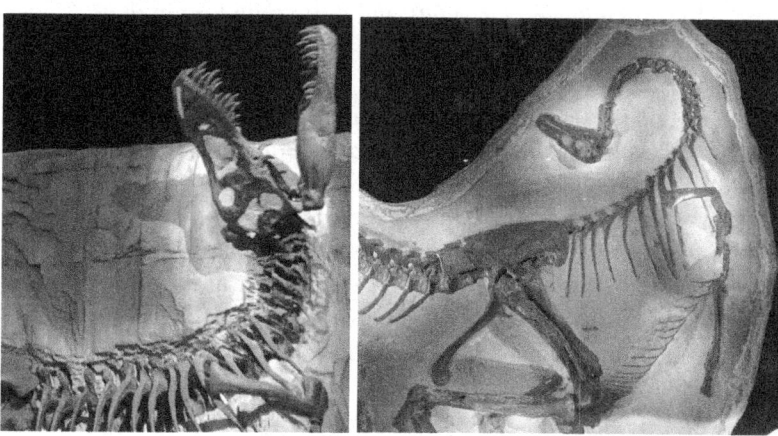

Figure 29. Dinosaurs in the Common "Death Pose," Indicating Rapid Burial and Suffocation (Royal Tyrrell Museum, Author).

Yet another clue that the dinosaurs were wiped out catastrophically is the fact that so many are found buried simultaneously, fleeing in groups. For example, Figure 30 plots both the sauropod and triceratops dinosaur fossils that have been found in the Midwestern United States. Isn't it interesting that these totally different dinosaur types were simultaneously wiped out and buried in the *same areas*? Something stopped these two very large dinosaur types dead in their tracks and buried them in mud, preserving their fossils for us to find today.

Sauropod Fossils in the Midwest

Triceratops Fossils in the Midwest

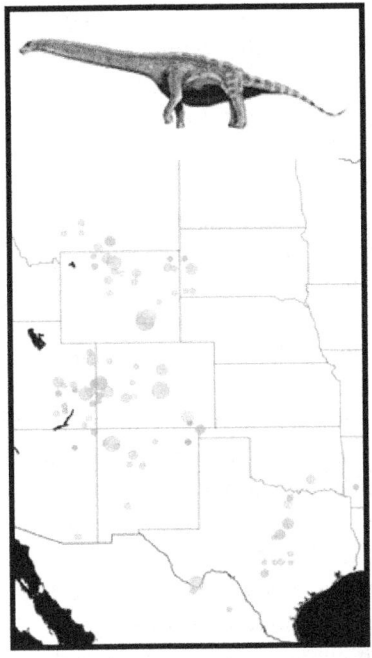
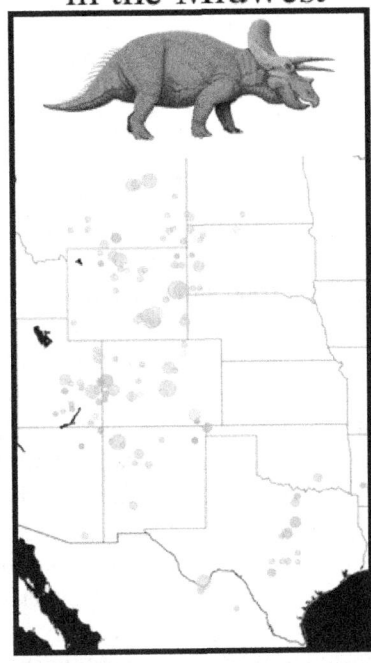

Figure 30. Sauropod and *Triceratops* Graveyards.[101]

Sauropods and *Triceratops* are some of the largest dinosaurs to ever live. What type of event would it take to bury these massive creatures in mud so quickly that they would be disarticulated and preserved for us to find today—locked in mud that hardened into rock before getting scavenged? Slow, gradually rising creeks or rivers? A sudden worldwide Flood fits the evidence much better.

Let's drill down and take a look at one of the largest mass dinosaur graves in the world found at Dinosaur Provincial Park in Canada. In just this one area, over 32,000 fossil specimens have been found, representing 35 species, 34 genera, and 12 families of dinosaurs. Astonishingly, dinosaur fossils intermingle with fish, turtles, marsupials and other mammals, and amphibians. Also, only 300 complete animals have been found! The large majority were scrambled, pulverized, and blended together, as if the world became an enormous washing machine.

There are 14 mega bone beds at this location that collectively contain thousands of buried *Centrosaurus* found in the same stratigraphic column (a term used in geology to describe the vertical sequence of rocks in a particular area). The authors who completed the most extensive study of the area described the sediment in which these dinosaurs are buried as "mudstone rich in organic matter deposited on the tract of land separating two ancient rivers."[102] They also concluded that each of the 14 bone beds was actually part of a single, massive "mega-bone bed" that occupied 2.3 square kilometers—almost a square mile! Stop and think about this for a minute. How did thousands of dinosaurs—of the same species—get herded up and simultaneously buried in mud?

These authors even concluded that the massive bone beds were formed when a herd of *Centrosaurus* drowned during a flood. These bone beds are also found with aquatic vertebrates such as fish, turtles, and crocodiles, showing that water was definitely involved in their transport and burial. In addition, almost no teeth marks indicated little scavenging after these animals died, probably because most of them died at the same time.[103]

While visiting this location, one outdoor display caught my daughter's eye. It was a large hadrosaur, a "duck-bill" dinosaur, that they left in the ground, exactly as it was found, covered with mud and twisted around like it went through a blender before it was buried. A young boy pushed a button to play the audio explanation provided by the museum that described the evolutionary idea about how the animal died. They explained that a large tropical storm caused the rivers to rise and the dinosaurs to drown—one after the other—as each blindly followed the other to their death (thousands of them).[104]

This is when my daughter had her epiphany: "You've got to be kidding me!" she exclaimed. "Look at all these dead dinosaurs—they're everywhere! And they're buried in countless tons of sediment—how's a local rainstorm going to do that? Noah's Flood is a much better explanation!" She's onto something. If rainstorms explain this, then why don't they deposit and fossilize even smaller creatures today? This 2.3 square kilometer dinosaur graveyard was massive—how much mudflow did the Flood have to bring onto land to bury over 10,000 *Centrosaurus*?[105]

Other dinosaur mass gravesites exist around the world. An online article on *Discovery.com* describes a dinosaur graveyard in China as the largest in the world, writing, "Researchers say they can't understand why so many animals gathered in what is today the city of Zhucheng to die." Thousands of dinosaur bones stack on top of each other in "incredible density," then they "suddenly vanished from the face of the Earth."[106] Most of the bones are found within a single 980-foot-long ravine in the Chinese countryside, about 415 miles southeast of Beijing. Clearly, processes were going on in the past that were so violent they are hardly imaginable.

A dinosaur mass grave in Montana unveils yet more evidence for rapid burial during Noah's Flood. In his article titled, "The Extinction of the Dinosaurs," Creation researcher and meteorologist Michael Oard describes some of the numerous dinosaur graveyards that are found all over the world.[107] He believes this is solid evidence of Noah's worldwide Flood. Oard reported that one of the largest bone beds in the world is located in north-central Montana:

> Based on outcrops, an extrapolated estimate was made for 10,000 duckbill dinosaurs entombed in a thin layer measuring 2 km east-west and 0.5 km north-south. The bones are disarticulated and disassociated, and are orientated east-west. However, a few bones were standing upright, indicating some type of debris flow. Moreover, there are no young juveniles or babies in this bone-bed, and the bones are all from one species of dinosaur.

Oard concluded that a cataclysmic event is the best explanation for the arrangement of the bones. Two leading secular scientists, Horner and Gorman, also described the bone bed: "How could any mud slide, no matter how catastrophic, have the force to take a two- or three-ton animal that had just died and smash it around so much that its femur—still embedded in the flesh of its thigh—split lengthwise?"[108]

Figure 31 shows the text from books or articles about the particular fossil graveyard shown. Isn't it incredible that everyone admits that some type of watery catastrophe was responsible for piling up the dinosaurs into these mass graves?

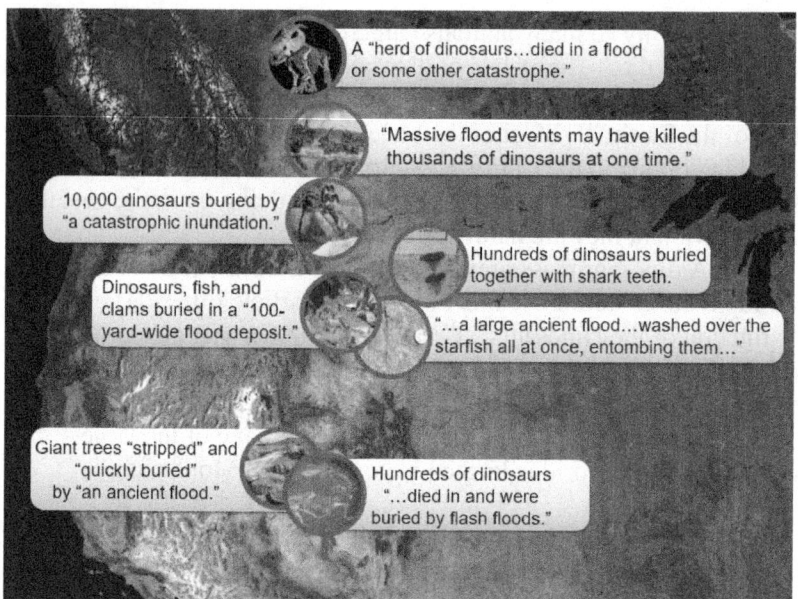

Figure 31. Dinosaur Graveyards in Midwestern U.S. with "Flood Catastrophe" Explanations from Secular Sources.[109]

Dinosaur Soft Tissue

Some would argue that the case for Biblical Creation would grow stronger if a living dinosaur was found in an unexplored swamp in the Congo. In actuality, however, what scientists have found over the last 20 years regarding soft tissue is even more convincing than discovering a living dinosaur.

You see, if someone found a living dinosaur somewhere, it would be easy for evolutionists to explain away—holding that evolution was on "idle" for eons. They've already done this many times when so-called "living fossils" are found, such as the coelacanth that someone hauled up in a fishing net off Madagascar in 1938. Before they found it alive, coelacanths were considered a key "missing link" between fish and amphibians, dating back to the time of the dinosaurs and beyond.[110]

So the reason that the discovery of dinosaur biomolecules, cells, and tissues is *even better* than finding a living dinosaur is that the laws of chemistry hold evolutionists accountable for claiming either that thermodynamics—the process by which tissues break down—was idle for eons or, even more far out, that the bio-organic materials are *not even there*. Knowing these bio-organic materials were present when they were living, and still having them now, provides undeniable evidence for Noah's Flood staring the world in the face.

This is why the recent discovery of 16 different types of short-lived dinosaur biomaterials that remain in dinosaur bones and other body parts like skin and horns is so important. Decay experiments have placed outer limits on how long they should last before completely decaying. For each of these materials, their "expiration date" is well before 65 million years, which is when dinosaurs supposedly went extinct. So, rather than being 65 million years old, these materials are just thousands of years old. The science of protein decay fits the Bible's timeline of dinosaurs recently buried in Noah's Flood.

Secular scientists have published each of these dinosaur-era fresh biomaterials in peer-reviewed, evolution-based science journals. One of most frequently used "rescuing devices" that is given by evolutionists to try to explain some of these findings is "bacterial contamination." However, microbes do not produce *any* of the biomaterials covered below, ruling out recent contamination.

Many dinosaur bones are even found **un-fossilized** in places like Madagascar, Alaska, and Montana (see the section below titled, "Fresh Dinosaur Biomaterial #7: Unmineralized Bone"). Even the founder of the largest dinosaur museum in the world admitted that "…usually most of the original bone is still present in a dinosaur fossil."[111] Sadly, most students who attend public schools today develop the opinion that dinosaur bones are just rock impressions of bones. Nothing could be further from the truth!

Fresh Dinosaur Biomaterial #1: Blood Vessels

Blood vessels transport blood throughout the body. They include the tiny capillaries, through which water and chemicals pass between blood and the tissue. Bones include capillaries and larger vessels. Small, pancake-shaped cells loaded with long-lasting collagen protein comprise blood vessels.

The blood vessels shown in Figure 32 were discovered when Dr. Mary Schweitzer's team was attempting to move a gigantic *Tyrannosaurus rex* fossil by helicopter that turned out to be too heavy. They were forced to break apart the leg bone. When looking at the inside of the leg bone at the lab, they discovered that the inside of the bone was partially hollow (not mineralized), revealing the soft tissue shown in Figure 32 that was extracted after treatments to remove the minerals.[112]

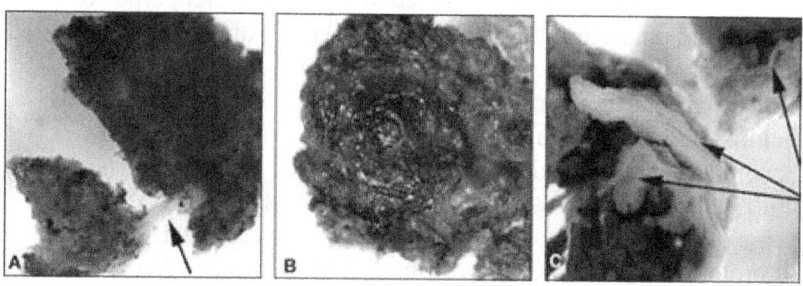

Figure 32. Tissue Fragments from a *T. rex* Femur.[113]

The tissues that are shown on the left of Figure 32 show that it is flexible and resilient. When stretched, it returned to its original shape. The middle photo shows the bone after it was air dried. The photo at right shows regions of bone showing fibrous tissue, not normally seen in fossil bone.

Since this publication in 2005, blood vessels from several other dinosaurs and other extinct reptiles have been described and published in numerous leading scientific journals, including the *Annals of Anatomy*, *Science* (the leading journal of the American Association for the Advancement of Science), *Public Library of Sciences ONE*, and the *Proceedings from the Royal Society B*, which focuses on the biological sciences.[114]

Fresh Dinosaur Biomaterial #2: Red Blood Cells

Red blood cells carry oxygen and collect carbon dioxide using hemoglobin protein—also found in dinosaur and other fossils. Dr. Mary Schweitzer was one of the first to discover and publish the discovery of red blood cells, which she shares in her own words: "The lab filled with murmurs of amazement, for I had focused on something inside the vessels that none of us had ever noticed before: tiny round objects, translucent red with a dark center. Then a colleague took one look at them and shouted, 'You've got red blood cells. You've got red blood cells!'"[115]

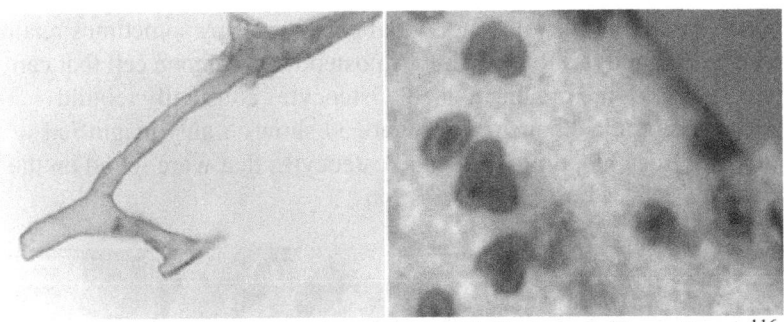

Figure 33. Blood Vessels and Red Blood Cells from a *T. rex* Bone.[116]

These two photos in Figure 33 are from a 2005 discovery from Dr. Schweitzer that clearly show blood vessels from a *T. rex* bone (left) and red blood cells (right). How could these cells last for 65 million years? At least five peer-reviewed scientific journals have published accounts of red blood cells in dinosaur and other fossil bones.[117]

Regarding this discovery, Dr. Schweitzer remarked, "If you take a blood sample, and you stick it on a shelf, you have nothing recognizable in about a week. So why would there be anything left in dinosaurs?"[118] That's certainly a good question, and one that has an easier answer if dinosaur fossils are only thousands of years old!

Fresh Dinosaur Biomaterial #3: Hemoglobin

Hemoglobin protein contains iron and transports oxygen in red blood cells of most vertebrates. Some invertebrates, including certain insects and some worms, also use hemoglobin. In vertebrates, this amazing protein picks up oxygen from lungs or gills and carries it to the rest of the body's cells. There, oxygen fuels aerobic respiration by which cells produce energy.

Scientific studies have reported "striking evidence for the presence of hemoglobin derived peptides in the [*T. rex*] bone extract"[119] and several other dinosaur "era" bones.[120]

Fresh Dinosaur Biomaterial #4: Bone Cells (Osteocytes)

Secular scientists have described dinosaur proteins like hemoglobin, even though no experimental evidence supports the possibility that they can last for even a million years. But dinosaur bones hold more than just individual proteins. They sometimes retain whole cells and tissue remnants. An osteocyte is a bone cell that can live as long as the organism itself. Osteocytes constantly rebuild bones and regulate bone mass. Figure 34 shows highly magnified blood vessels, blood products, and osteocytes that were found on the inside of a brow horn of a *Triceratops*.

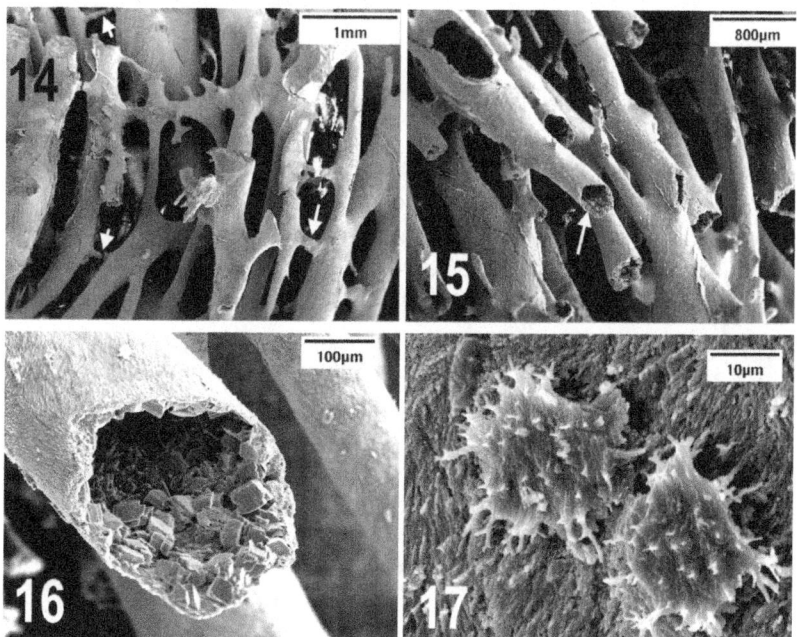

Figure 34. Soft Bone Material from a Brow Horn of a *Triceratops horridus* from Montana.[121]

Figure 34 shows blood vessels linked together (white arrows in frame 14). Frame 15 shows possible blood products lining inner wall of hardened vessel (white arrow). Frame 16 is enlarged from frame 15 and shows crystallized nature of possible blood products lining inner wall of hardened vessel. Frame 17 shows two large oblate osteocytes lying on fibrillar bone matrix.

At least four scientific studies have established osteocytes in dinosaur bones. One study even found nucleic acid signatures consistent with ancient DNA right where the nucleus would have been in dinosaur osteocytes.[122]

Fresh Dinosaur Biomaterial #5: Ovalbumin (Proteins)

Another protein found in fossils that microbes don't make is called ovalbumin. It makes up 60–65% of the total protein in egg whites. Ovalbumin has been found in exceptionally preserved sauropod eggs discovered in Patagonia, Argentina, a dig site that included skeletal remains and soft tissues of embryonic titanosaurid dinosaurs. These findings were reported in a peer-reviewed scientific journal.[123]

Fresh Dinosaur Biomaterial #6: Chitin

Chitin is a biochemical found in squid beaks and pens, arthropod exoskeletons, and certain fungi. If chitin was meant to last for millions of years, then it might have filled Earth's surface as dead insects, krill, and fungi left their remains over eons. Chitin is tough, but no known experiment supplies any reason to so much as suspect that it could last a million years, let alone hundreds of millions. Yet, at least two scientific studies report finding it in ancient fossils (dinosaur "era" and beyond).[124] Our Creator equipped many microbes with unique enzymes that digest chitin, so what could have kept those microbes away from all that chitin for millions of years?

Fresh Dinosaur Biomaterial #7: Unmineralized Bone

Fresh-looking, un-mineralized dinosaur bones pop up in dig sites around the world. In Alaska, for example, a petroleum geologist working for Shell Oil Company discovered well-preserved bones in Alaska along the Colville River. The bones looked so fresh that he assumed these were recently deposited, perhaps belonging to a mammoth or bison. Twenty years later scientists recognized them as *Edmontosaurus* bones—a duck-billed dinosaur.[125]

Figure 35. Unfossilized *Hadrosaur* Bone from the Liscomb Bone Bed.[126]

Mineralized bones can look darker than bone and typically feel quite heavy. Un-mineralized bones retain their original structure, often including the tiny pore spaces in spongy bone, as shown in Figure 35. One study includes an interesting section that states:

> Finally, a two-part mechanism, involving first cross-linking of molecular components and subsequent mineralization, is proposed to explain the surprising presence of still-soft elements in fossil bone. These results suggest that present models of fossilization processes may be incomplete and that *soft tissue elements may be more commonly preserved, even in older specimens, than previously thought.*[127] Additionally, in many cases, osteocytes with defined nuclei are preserved, and may represent an important source for informative molecular data (emphasis added).

Numerous other studies published in scientific journals have described these un-mineralized dinosaur bone findings.[128]

Sometimes evolutionists are surprised by the fact that many dinosaur bones contain "fresh," original bone. It seems that decades of conditioning that "dinosaur bones become solid rocks" and ideas of "millions of years" have framed assumptions that are frequently being broken today.

However, researchers out in the field—actually digging up bones—oftentimes have a different viewpoint. Take Dr. Mary Schweitzer's testimony for example, where she notes that many "fresh" dinosaur bones still have the stench of death:

> This shifting perspective clicked with Schweitzer's intuitions that dinosaur remains were more than chunks of stone. Once, when she was working with a *T. rex* skeleton harvested from Hell Creek, she noticed that the fossil exuded a distinctly organic odor. "It smelled just like one of the cadavers we had in the lab who had been treated with chemotherapy before he died," she says. Given the conventional wisdom that such fossils were made up entirely of minerals, Schweitzer was anxious when mentioning this to Horner [a leading paleontologist]. "But he said, 'Oh, yeah, all Hell Creek bones smell,'" she says. To most old-line paleontologists, the smell of death didn't even register. To Schweitzer, it meant that traces of life might still cling to those bones.[129]

Experienced dinosaur fossil collectors have developed similar opinions. Take experienced dinosaur hunter and wholesaler, Alan Stout, for example. Alan Stout is a long-time fossil collector and has collected and sold millions of dollars' worth of dinosaur specimens to collectors, researchers, and museums worldwide.[130] After collecting in Montana's Hell Creek formation (and surrounding areas) for over a decade, Alan states that many of the dinosaur bones he finds in the Cretaceous layers are only 40% mineralized, with as much as 60% of the bone being original material. He even notes that some of the fossils "look just like they were buried yesterday after scraping off just the outside layer of mineralization."[131]

Fresh Dinosaur Biomaterial #8: Collagen

Collagen is the main structural protein found in animal connective tissue. When boiled, collagen turns into gelatin, showing its sensitivity to temperature. In 2007, scientists discovered collagen amino acid sequences from a *T. rex* fossil that supposedly dated at 68 million years. Met with controversy, some suggested these proteins came from lab workers who accidentally contaminated the samples being studied. Or perhaps traces of ostrich bone proteins lingered in the equipment used in the study. Some even said, well perhaps "a bird died on top of the *T. rex* excavation site."[132] However, three separate labs verified collagen in dinosaurs in 2009[133] and again in January 2017.[134] The 2017 study even confirmed the collagen at the *molecular level*, and stated, "We are confident that the results we obtained are not contamination and that this collagen is original to the specimen."[135]

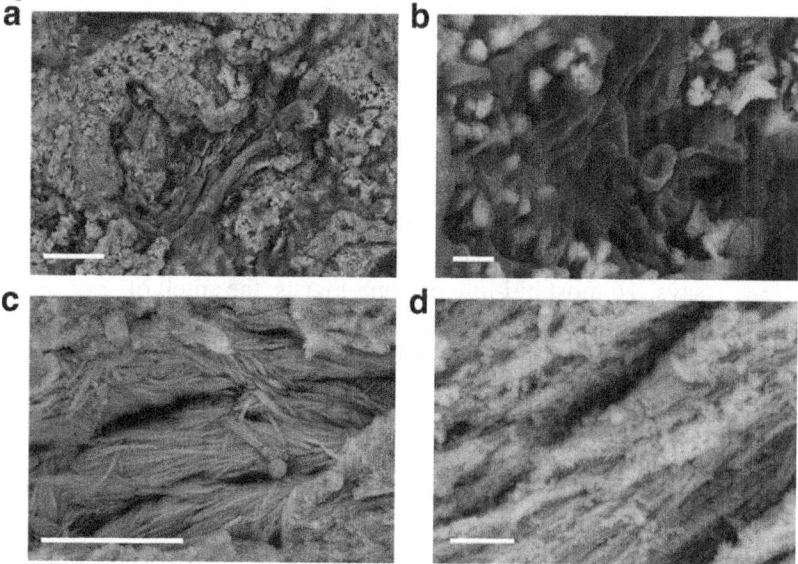

Figure 36. Fibers and Cellular Structures in Dinosaur Specimens.[136]

Experiments have projected that the absolute theoretical maximum life of collagen ranges from 300,000 to 900,000 years under the best possible conditions.[137] This shows that collagen proteins should not last one million years, but could (in the absence of microbes) last for thousands of years. This confronts millions-of-years age assignments for dinosaur remains, but is consistent with the biblical time frame of thousands of years.

However, the rescuing devices being offered by evolutionists are not far behind. For example, in a recent article published in *Science*, Dr. Schweitzer tried to explain how the collagen sequences supposedly survived tens of millions of years: "... as red blood cells decay after an animal dies, iron liberated from their hemoglobin may react with nearby proteins, linking them together. This crosslinking, she says, causes proteins to precipitate out of solution, drying them out in a way that helps preserve them." Critical of this idea, however, Dr. Matthew Collins, a paleoproteomics expert at the University of York in the United Kingdom, stated that he doesn't think that the process described by Dr. Schweitzer could "arrest protein degradation for tens of millions of years, so he, for one, remains skeptical of Schweitzer's claim: 'Proteins decay in an orderly fashion. We can slow it down, but not by a lot.'"[138]

Fresh Dinosaur Biomaterial #9: DNA (Limited)

One measured decay rate of DNA, extracted from recently deposited fossil bird bones, showed a half-life of 521 years. DNA decays quickly. It should have spontaneously decayed into smaller chemicals after several tens of thousands of years—and it could only last that long if kept cool. A few brave secular scientists have reported DNA structures from dinosaur bones, although they did not directly address the question of its age.[139]

Fresh Dinosaur Biomaterial #10: Skin Pigments

In 2008, a group of paleontologists found exceptionally well-preserved *Psittacosaurus* remains in China and published images of dinosaur collagen fiber bundles. Other scientists published stunning skin color images from a separate *Psittacosaurus*, also from China, and found evidence of original, unaltered pigments including carotenoids and melanins. Nobody has performed an experiment that so much as suggests these pigments could last a million years. Still other studies have reported scaled skin and hemoglobin decay products—still colored red, as were some of Dr. Mary Schweitzer's *T. rex* and hadrosaurine samples—in a Kansas mosasaur.[140]

The latest findings continue to confirm the recent demise of most of the dinosaurs by a massive Flood. Consider this 3,000-pound nodosaur fossil just found in Canada shown in Figure 37. Evolutionists date this fossil at 110 million years old. But how did everything stay intact for so long? Skin pigment, guts, scales, full boney armor, keratin—even its last meal was found in its stomach! Paleobiologist Jakob Vinther said, "The dinosaur is so well preserved that it 'might have been walking around a couple of weeks ago, I've never seen anything like this."[141] Rather than being scavenged after death, this dinosaur was rapidly entombed by Noah's Flood just thousands of years ago.

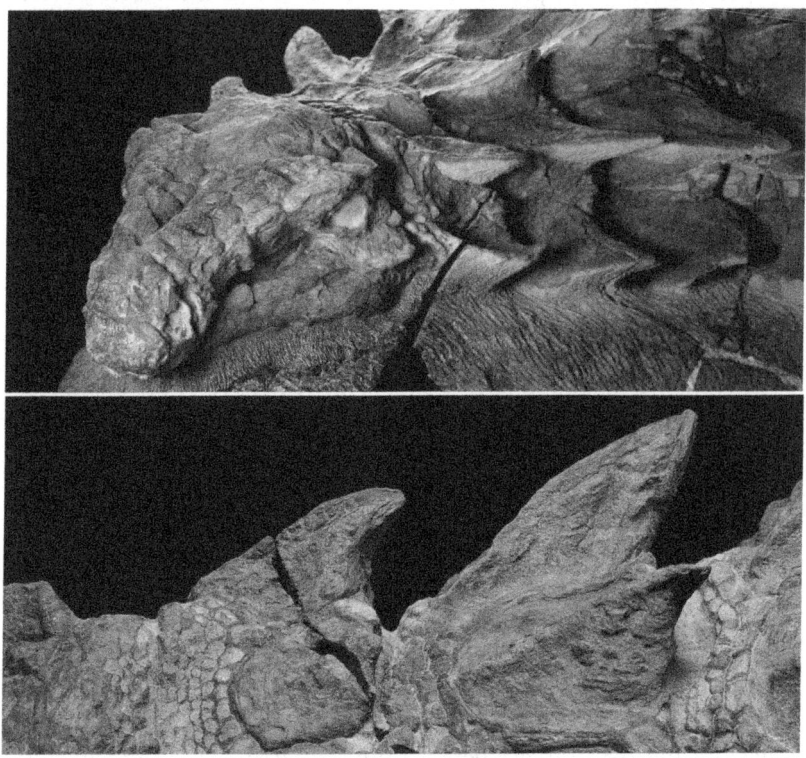

Figure 37. Nodosaur Fossil with Fossilized Skin.[142]

Fresh Dinosaur Biomaterial #11: PHEX (Proteins)

PHEX is a protein involved in bone mineralization in mammals. In 2013, Dr. Mary Schweitzer published detailed findings of the soft, transparent microstructures her team found in dinosaur bones. Because this discovery was so controversial, her team used advanced mass spectrometry techniques to confirm the findings. Other methods demonstrated that proteins such as actin, tubulin, and PHEX found in osteocytes from two different dinosaurs were not from some form of contamination but came from the creatures' remains.[143]

Fresh Dinosaur Biomaterial #12: Histone H4 (Proteins)

Bacteria do not make histone H4, but animals do. DNA wraps around it like a spool. Dr. Mary Schweitzer and her team found this protein inside a hadrosaur femur found in the Hell Creek Formation in Montana, which bears an assigned age of 67 million years. It might last for thousands of years if kept sterile, but no evidence so much as hints that it could last for a million years.[144]

Fresh Dinosaur Biomaterial #13: Keratin (Structural Protein)

Keratin forms the main structural constituent of hair, feathers, hooves, claws, and horns. Some modern lizard skins contain tiny disks of keratin embedded in their scales. Researchers identified keratin protein in fossilized lizard skin scales from the Green River Formation that supposedly date to 50 million years ago. They explained its presence with a story about clay minerals attaching to the keratin to hold it in place for all that time. However, water would have to deposit the clay, and water helps rapidly degrade keratin. The most scientifically responsible explanation should be the simplest one—that this fossil is thousands, not millions, of years old.[145] Other fossils with original keratin include *Archaeopteryx*[146] bird feather residue and stegosaur spikes.[147]

Fresh Dinosaur Biomaterial #14: Elastin

Elastin is a highly elastic protein found in connective tissue, skin, and bones. It helps body parts resume their shape after stretching or contracting, like when skin gets poked or pinched. Bacteria don't need it or make it, and elastin should not last a million years, even in the best preservation environment. Scientists reported finding this protein in a hadrosaur femur found in Montana.[148]

Fresh Dinosaur Biomaterial #15: Cartilage

A 2020 article in a peer-reviewed science journal reports[149] a discovery that was so astounding the lead scientist said, "I couldn't believe it, my heart almost stopped beating." What was the finding?

Soft dinosaur cartilage with *original molecules* still present. To remove any doubt that what they were seeing was real, they ran additional laboratory tests that supported "the presence of remnants of original cartilaginous proteins in this dinosaur."

In one bone fragment they noticed some "exquisitely preserved cells within preserved calcified cartilage tissues on the edges of a bone" with two cartilage cells still linked together by an intercellular bridge, which is consistent with the end of cell division (see left image below). The image also reveals dark material resembling a cell nucleus. One cartilage cell also had dark, elongated structures that were "morphologically consistent with chromosomes" (center image below).

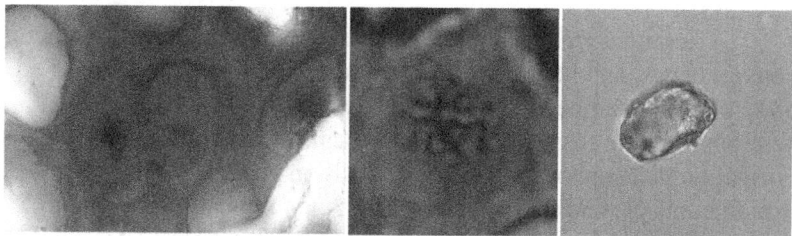

Figure 38. Dinosaur Cartilage.[150]

Fresh Dinosaur Biomaterial #16: Nerves

In 2021, in-tact nerves were found inside of a *Triceratops* occipital condyle, which is a hard, round-shaped bone that protrudes from the base of the skull that mounts to the end of the spine—just like a trailer ball-and-hitch design.[151]

Dr. Armitage compared this discovery with nerves from a chicken (see below) and demonstrated that the structures from the fossil have all the physical characteristics of modern chicken nerves, indicating they really are nerves from a vertebrate animal (not contaminants).

The white bars in the image below show the scale in micrometers (millionths of a meter). The pattern of dark lines wrapping around the chicken nerve on the left form a sheath that wraps around the bundle of fibers which makes up the nerve. The image on the right (from the *Triceratops*) shows the same pattern. How is that for a bone that is supposedly millions of years old?

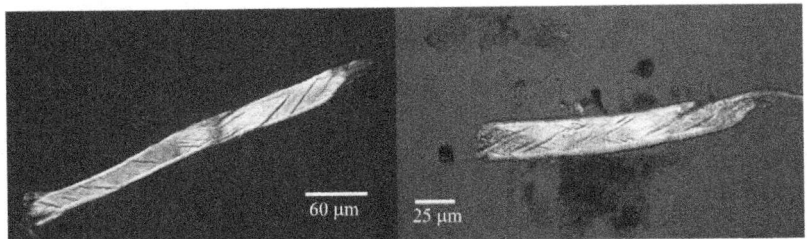

Figure 39. Dinosaur Nerves. A nerve from a chicken (left) compared to one isolated from a dinosaur fossil (right).[152]

Making this even more convincing, Dr. Armitage took steps to ensure that these nerves were not "petrified structures" of a nerve, but were *actually the nerves themselves*. This was done by decalcifying the bone, leaving soft tissues behind: "The flexibility of individual decalcified nerves was astonishing. Nerves held at each end with fine needle forceps only broke into two pieces after repeated tugging. An example of the flexibility of these nerves … where the fascicle rotates through a gentle, unbroken loop and descends into other curvatures before terminating to a point."

Biomaterial Summary

Because these findings are game changers, they are not without challenge by those who hold strongly to evolutionary ideas. Some of the rescuing devices that have been offered to attempt to explain these findings include iron in the blood acting as a preservative, the material being mistaken from a bird carcass mixed with the fossil, laboratory contamination, and even microbial biofilm (from bacteria in the bones). These explanations show an eagerness to attempt to dismiss the findings while clinging to the belief in millions of years. Rather than questioning the supposed long ages needed to prop up the evolutionary view, they seek other explanations to explain the presence of these materials, desperately denying the obvious.

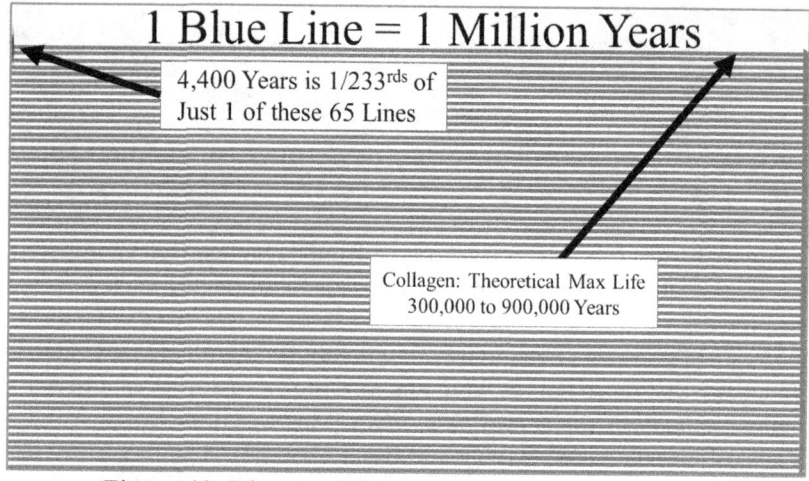

Figure 40. Dinosaur Biomaterials Time Comparison.

    Figure 40 shows a simulated timeline to attempt to put these findings into perspective. Each of these 65 lines represents 1 million years. Showing 4,400 years on this chart is difficult, but is represented by a tiny dot in the upper left, which is 1/233rds of just one of these lines, or less than one-half of 1 percent of one of these lines. While this assumption can never be tested, some studies have measured an absolute theoretical maximum life of between 300,000 and 900,000 years.[153] If these dinosaur bones are really 65 million years old (and older), this collagen lasted for *72 to 217 times longer than these measured and extrapolated maximum collagen shelf lives.* Does believing these materials could last that long require strong faith?

    Is it really possible that all 16 of these biomaterials lasted for 65 million years? Or, were they recent deposits that were quickly sealed in Noah's Flood only thousands of years ago? You can decide, but one thing stands for certain: Given the positions that scientists have held for decades on bio-organic decay rates, all 16 of the materials discussed above clearly and easily—without any academic caveats—**fit the Genesis timeline just fine.** But they don't fit the 65 million-year timeline without severe **academic torture.**

    In the words of paleontologist Dr. Mary Schweitzer: "What really bothers people is: Why the heck is this stuff there…A lot of people aren't willing to accept the data until we come up with a mechanism for preservation…We're not there yet. All I can say is:

Here's what we see, here's what we've done, and here's our results."[154] Evidence abounds showing the extreme resistance of secular institutions accepting the implications of dinosaur soft tissue. An article in *Discover* magazine[155] documented that Dr. Schweitzer "was having a hard time" trying to get her soft tissue dinosaur evidence published in scientific journals. Dr. Schweitzer stated, "I had one reviewer tell me that he didn't care what the data said, he knew that what I was finding wasn't possible." When Dr. Schweitzer wrote back asking, "Well, what data would convince you?" the reviewer stated, "None." Professor Mark Armitage was actually fired from his position at a university after publishing the soft tissue results he found in *Triceratops* horn.[156]

The fact that many dinosaur fossils are not "just rocks," but are actually still bones, should alone move most reasonable minds out of the "millions of years" framework. But the fact that evolutionists have somehow excluded the realities of biological decay from dinosaur bones is also actually quite telling from both scientific and theological perspectives (2 Peter 3 and Romans 1). Rather than accepting the obvious conclusion that the bones are only thousands of years old—not millions—many continue to work fiercely to find ways to stretch the dinosaur fossil record out millions of years beyond what the obvious evidence points to. Rather than shortening the timeline to fit the obvious conclusion suggested by the presence of the 16 bio-organic materials, many work feverishly to find ways to stretch the decay rates out to over 100 times longer than the present science shows they can last (as in the case with collagen, discussed above).

Does the Fossil Record Show Transitional Forms?

Dr. Carl Werner and his wife Debbie invested over 14 years of their lives investigating "the best museums and dig sites around the globe [and] photographing thousands of original fossils and the actual fossil layers where they were found."[157] After visiting hundreds of museums and interviewing hundreds of paleontologists, scientists, and museum curators, Dr. Werner concluded: "Now, 150 years after Darwin wrote his book, this problem still persists. Overall, the fossil record is rich—200 million fossils in museums—but the predicted evolutionary ancestors are missing, seemingly contradicting evolution."[158] He continues with a series of examples:

- Museums have collected the fossil remains of 100,000 individual dinosaurs, but have not found a single direct ancestor for any dinosaur species.
- Approximately 200,000 fossil birds have been found, but ancestors of the oldest birds have yet to be discovered.
- The remains of 100,000 fossilized turtles have been collected by museums, yet the direct ancestors of turtles are missing.
- Nearly 1,000 flying reptiles (pterosaurs) have been collected, but no ancestors showing ground reptiles evolving into flying reptiles have been found.
- Over 1,000 fossil bats have been collected by museums, but no ancestors have been found showing a ground mammal slowly evolving into a flying mammal.
- Approximately 500,000 fossil fish have been collected, and 100,000,000 invertebrates have been collected, but ancestors for the theoretical first fish—a series of fossils showing an invertebrate changing into a fish—are unknown.
- Over 1,000 fossil sea lions have been collected, but not a single ancestor of sea lions has been found.
- Nearly 5,000 fossilized seals have been collected, but not a single ancestor has been found.

Dinosaur Fossil Transitions and Ancestors

While doing his research, Dr. Werner noted, "If evolution was not true, and if animals did not change over time, I should be able to find modern-appearing plants and modern-appearing animals in the dinosaur rock layers. And this is in fact what I found." Dr. Werner has documented 432 mammal species in the dinosaur fossil layers. After visiting 60 museums around the world, he did not find a single complete mammal skeleton from the dinosaur layers displayed at **any** of these museums. Some mammals are even found in the stomachs of dinosaurs! These mammals are missing because they don't fit the evolutionary story represented by most museums, where the "mammal" era follows after the "dinosaur" era. The fact is that hundreds of mammal species are found buried with dinosaurs.

Mixed in among dinosaurs Dr. Werner found "all of today's reptile groups" as well as **birds**. How does this work if dinosaurs supposedly evolved into birds as evolutionists claim? Something's not lining up with evolution theory! In fact, at least 120 bird species[159] have been found buried alongside the dinosaurs, including numerous "modern" looking birds like loons, parrots, flamingos, cormorants, sandpipers, owls, penguins, avocets, ducks, and numerous waterfowl.[160] Dinosaur footprints have also been found right alongside bird footprints.[161] The fact is that birds have existed alongside land creatures since the creation week.

Leading dinosaur expert Dr. Weishample wrote this about dinosaur ancestors: "From my reading of the fossil record of dinosaurs, no direct ancestors have been discovered for **any** dinosaur species. Alas, my list of dinosaurian ancestors is an empty one."[162] This sure seems to match the Bible's account—God put them here, fully formed.

Consider pterosaurs—massive flying reptiles with wingspans sometimes over 40 feet that could possibly only fly in the pre-Flood world.[163] Dr. Viohl, Curator of the Famous Jura Museum in Germany said, "We know only little about the evolution of pterosaurs. The ancestors are not known... When the pterosaurs first appear in the geologic record, they were completely perfect. They were perfect pterosaurs."[164] After finding so many specimens in complete form, shouldn't *some* predecessors have been found by now?

Figure 41 shows the widespread distribution of pterosaur fossils around the world. Isn't it interesting that they are found everywhere? But that's not the only thing—they're found in every fossil layer from what evolutionists refer to as the Mesozoic Era (from the Late Triassic to Late Cretaceous, spanning from 228 to 66 million years ago in the evolutionary timeline). Is it possible that they are found in these different major rock units because—as flyers—they had the best chance of surviving the longest during the Flood to escape to safer areas as the Flood unfolded?

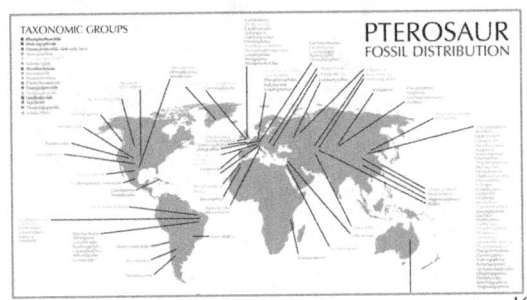

Figure 41. Pterosaur Fossil Distribution Map.[165]

If museums have over 1,000 fossilized pterosaurs, why haven't they found any fossils that have been classified as "pre-pterosaurs"? Why are pterosaurs always found in complete form? Where are the transitional fossils that should exist if evolution theory is true?

Perhaps this explains why the evolutionary ideas about dinosaur ancestors keep changing—especially when they've now found dinosaurs even buried alongside their supposed ancestors.[166] After Dr. Werner interviewed dozens of leading dinosaur experts from museums across the globe about dinosaur ancestors and transitions, he summarized his findings on this chart from the Chicago Field Museum.

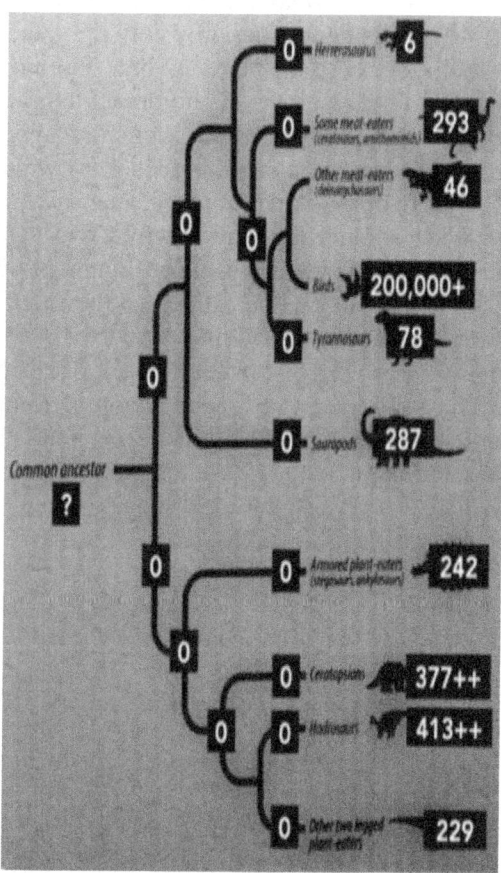

Figure 42. Dinosaur "Transitions."[167]

Note the counts of the different dinosaur varieties found—for example, the 78 *T. rex* specimens. Think about it—if over 100,000 dinosaurs have been collected by museums and dinosaurs evolved from one type into another as theorized on the chart, shouldn't there be counts on the nodes of these supposed branches between dinosaur kinds? Instead, this chart just demonstrates what we would expect if creation is true: the counts of the individual types of creatures found, with zero transitions.

It's also amazing when you look at the creatures on this chart that are supposedly evolving from the same branch, yet they are so obviously different—like *Ankylosaurus* and *Triceratops*. They've never found a single creature that looks anything like an earlier version of either of these dinosaurs, or one that looks like some hybrid of the two of them.

Figure 43. *Ankylosaurus* and *Triceratops* in the same evolutionary branch? If they both come from a supposed common ancestor, where are all the millions of transitional design changes it would take to go from one to the other?

With hundreds of these creatures found in their existing form—and always found in these forms—it becomes clear that the evolution of dinosaurs is a far, far reach. If they both come from a supposed common ancestor, where are all the millions of transitional design changes it would take to go from one of these creatures to the other? Yet not a single such creature has ever been found.

The chart in Figure 44 was reproduced from *The Encyclopedia of Dinosaurs* published in association with the British Museum of Natural History.[168] In small print at the bottom it says: "Tinted areas indicate solid fossil evidence." We've highlighted these in yellow (lighter shade on the tops of most bars if you're viewing this in black and white). The rest of the chart—shown in grey—shows the **theoretical** ideas about dinosaur ancestors and transitions in the dinosaur evolutionary tree. When the theoretical grey lines are removed (the imagined ancestors and transitions) all that remains are dinosaur "kinds" that were created in the beginning. Then, when the long ages are removed, you can see that these dinosaur kinds suddenly appeared together—by creation—on the sixth day of Creation Week. So much for dinosaur ancestors and transitions!

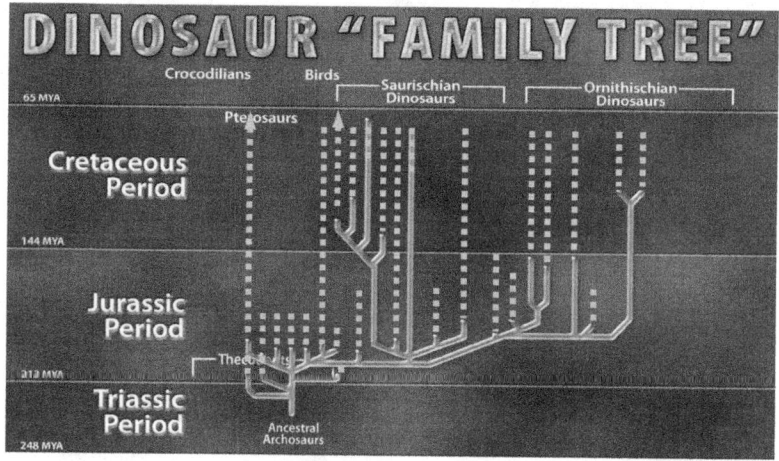

Figure 44. Dinosaur "Ancestors" and "Transitions."[169]

Summary

If this chapter was not enough, one more key consideration should clearly convince. What if, after countless millions of hours spent by researchers mining the crust of the Earth for fossil evidence, the fossil record is essentially *complete*? That is, it stands to reason that the millions of fossils we have collected over the last 150 years *exhaustively* record all basic life forms that ever lived, with only a few additional "big surprises" to be found. Given this, can we say that the question of transitional forms has been *asked and answered*?

One way to find out is to "calculate the percentage of those animals living today that have also been found as fossils. In other words, if the fossil record is comprised of a high percentage of animals that are living today, then the fossil record could be viewed as being fairly complete; that is, most animals that have lived on the Earth have been fossilized and discovered."[170] Carl Werner provides a chart demonstrating the results of such an investigation:[171]

- Of the 43 living land animal *orders*, such as carnivores, rodents, bats, and apes, nearly all, or 97.7%, have been found as fossils. This means that at least one example from each animal order has been collected as a fossil.
- Of the 178 living land animal *families*, such as dogs, bears, hyenas, and cats, 87.8% have been found in fossils.

Evolutionists have had their chance—over 150 years and millions of fossils—to prove themselves, and they have come up wanting. The theory has been weighed, tested, measured, and falsified. Aren't 200 million opportunities and one and one-half centuries enough time to answer the issue that *confounded* Darwin himself?

> Why, if species have descended from other species by fine gradations, do we not everywhere see innumerable transitional forms? Why is not all nature in confusion, instead of the species being, as we see them, well defined?...But, as by this theory innumerable transitional forms must have existed, why do we not find them embedded in countless numbers in the crust of the Earth?...But in the intermediate region, having intermediate conditions of life, why do we not now find closely-linking intermediate varieties? This difficulty for a long time quite confounded me.[172]

Noah's Flood: How Did People and Animals Disperse Around the World after the Flood?

After the Flood, God commanded humanity to "increase in number and fill the earth" (Genesis 9:1). As rebellious humans, we did the opposite: "Then they said, 'Come, let us build ourselves a city, with a tower that reaches to the heavens, so that we may make a name for ourselves and not be scattered over the face of the whole earth" (Genesis 11:4). About 100 years after the Flood, God responded to this disobedience by confusing our language and dispersing us from the Tower of Babel around the globe. This dispersal included between 78 and 100 people groups (and languages).[173]

Assuming the Babel dispersion is a true account, how did people spread across the globe when much of it is presently covered by water? The answer is quite simple: during the (single) Ice Age that began after the Flood and lasted for a few hundred years after, the ocean levels were between 100 and 140 meters lower[174] than they are today. This made *land bridges* and *ice bridges* that melting ice has since submerged. Also, in many cases (e.g., Hawaii, North America, Tahiti, and other locations) both humans and animals arrived by boat. For more about this topic, we recommend Bill Cooper's book, *After the Flood: The Early Post-flood History of Europe Traced Back to Noah*[175] and other resources by Answers in Genesis.[176]

How Did Vegetation Spread Rapidly after the Flood?

How did vegetation spread rapidly after the Flood so that all the varieties of animals could have enough food to survive? Two considerations help answer this question: (1) How could the plants grow fast enough for the thousands of animals getting off the Ark, reproducing rapidly, and needing food sources? (2) How could the seeds and plants disperse around the world after the world-wide Flood? Let's answer each of these questions.

How could the plants grow fast enough?

The most important part to consider when answering this question is that plants had 220 days to grow after the Flood. The Flood account reports that the water rose for 150 days before beginning to recede. They didn't leave the ark until 370 days after the Flood began.

This left up to 220 days (over seven months) for plants to regrow.[177] Vegetation grows fast with the right conditions. Different varieties of grass take only 5–30 days to grow. Winter wheat takes about 7–8 months to reach maturity, and spring wheat is mature in only four months. Many vegetables grow to maturity in less than two months (including arugula, spinach, carrots, broccoli, radishes, onions, cucumbers, many types of beans and leafy vegetables, and even some root vegetables). Noah also took many seed varieties with him to plant in the new world. God told him, "You are to take every kind of food that is to be eaten and store it away as food for you and for them." (Genesis 6:21)

How could the seeds and plants disperse around the world after the Flood?

God has engineered a *wide variety* of ways for distributing plant life. In addition to intentional planting, there are five main ways that seeds are dispersed from the parent plant: gravity, wind, ballistic, animals, and by water.

Gravity is perhaps the most obvious way: plants drop their ripe fruit (containing seed) below the plant, the seeds nest into the soil and grow around the radius of the parent plant. Apples, citrus, coconuts, and passionfruit are examples of gravity dispersal.

Dandelions are a well-known example of wind dispersal. A 2003 study at the University of Regensburg in Germany found that 99.5% of dandelion seeds land within 10 meters of their parent. Each seed is designed with a "parachute" structure that lifts the seed for typically a one-second flight.[178]

A less common dispersal method is ballistic dispersal. This occurs where the seed is forcefully ejected by explosive dehiscence of the fruit. For example, the *Hura crepitans* plant is even called the dynamite tree due to the sound of the fruit exploding. The explosions are powerful enough to throw the seed up to 100 meters.[179]

Plants that rely on water dispersal have seeds that can travel for extremely long distances (especially those seeds that have hard shells and float). Water lilies and some palm trees do this.

Animal seed dispersion is perhaps the most fascinating and includes three primary methods. Some seeds have small hooks on the surface of a burr, so they attach themselves to animal fur for dispersion. The more obvious method that animals disperse seed is by eating the fruit and later excreting the undigestible seeds to form new plants—sometimes far away from the parent plant (e.g., blackberries, cherries, and apples). Many rodents (such as squirrels) and some birds disperse seeds by hoarding the seeds in hidden dens. This method alone is responsible for over 90% of seed dispersion in some tropical rain forests.[180]

When it comes to Noah's Flood specifically, Ginger Allen reminds us that seeds only had to endure water for a maximum of just over nine months. She wrote, "those that had hitched a ride on large mats of vegetation or on carcasses could be germinating while protected from the harsh conditions," and, "Most plants could have survived outside the Ark upon floating rafts of vegetation as seeds and as debris that could have gone a long way toward propagation of at least some plant life in the post-Flood world."[181] Finally, Noah did not open the ark until the dove brought back a leaf. This way he knew the world was ready to support the animals.

Helpful Resources

Genesis Apologetics

Mobile App:
Search for the free "Genesis Apologetics" App in the iTunes or Google Play stores.

Free Books and Videos:
5th–10th Grade Students: *www.debunkevolution.com*
11th grade-College: *www.sevenmyths.com*

YouTube Channel:
Channel Name: Genesis Apologetics

Dinosaurs:
www.genesisapologetics.com/dinosaurs

Theistic Evolution
www.genesisapologetics.com/theistic

"Lucy" (leading human evolution icon):
www.genesisapologetics.com/lucy

Answers in Genesis
www.answersingenesis.org

Institute for Creation Research
www.icr.org

Creation Ministries International
www.creation.com

Evolution: The Grand Experiment
www.thegrandexperiment.com

Creation Website Search Tool
www.searchcreation.org

Prayer of Salvation

You're not here by accident—God *loves* you and He *knows* who you are like no one else. His Word says:

> Lord, You have searched me and known me. You know my sitting down and my rising up; you understand my thought afar off. You comprehend my path and my lying down, and are acquainted with all my ways. For there is not a word on my tongue, but behold, O Lord, You know it altogether. You have hedged me behind and before, and laid Your hand upon me. Such knowledge is too wonderful for me; It is high, I cannot attain it. (Psalm 139:1–6)

God loves you with an everlasting love, and with a love that can cover all of your transgressions—all that you have ever done wrong. But you have to repent of those sins and trust the Lord Jesus Christ for forgiveness. Your past is in the past. He wants to give you a new future and new hope.

But starting this new journey requires a step—a step of faith. God has already reached out to you as far as He can. By giving His Son to die for your sins on the Cross, He's done everything He can to reach out to you. The next step is yours to take, and this step requires faith to receive His Son, Jesus, into your heart. It also requires repentance (turning away) from sin–a surrendered heart that is willing to reject a sinful lifestyle. Many believers have a much easier time leaving sinful lifestyles after they fully trust Jesus and nobody else and nothing else. Along with forgiveness, the Holy Spirit enters your life when you receive Jesus, and He will lead you into a different lifestyle and way—a way that will lead to blessing, joy, patient endurance under trials, and eternal life with Him.

If you are ready to receive Him, then consider four key Biblical truths.

1. Acknowledge that your sin separates you from God. Most simply, sin is our failure to measure up to God's holiness and His righteous standards. We sin by things we do, choices we make, attitudes we show, and thoughts we entertain. We also sin when we fail to do right things or even think right

thoughts. The Bible also says that all people are sinners: "there is none righteous, not even one." No matter how good we try to be, none of us does right things all the time. The Bible is clear, "For all have sinned and come short of the glory of God" (Romans 3:23). Admit it. Agree with God on this one.
2. Our sins demand punishment—the punishment of death and separation from God. However, because of His great love, God sent His only Son Jesus to die for our sins: "God demonstrates His own love for us in this: While we were still sinners, Christ died for us" (Romans 5:8). For you to come to God, you have to get rid of your sin problem. But, in our own strength, not one of us can do this! You can't make yourself right with God by being a better person. Only God can rescue us from our sins. He is willing to do this, not because of anything you can offer Him, but **just because He loves you**! "He saved us, not because of righteous things we had done, but because of His mercy" (Titus 3:5).
3. It's only God's grace that allows you to come to Him—not your efforts to "clean up your life" or work your way to Heaven. You can't earn it. It's a free gift: "For it is by grace you have been saved, through faith—and this not from yourselves, it is the gift of God—not by works, so that no one can boast" (Ephesians 2:8–9). Will you accept this gift?
4. For you to come to God, the penalty for your sin must be paid. God's gift to you is His son, Jesus, who paid the debt for you when He died on the Cross. "For the wages of sin is death, but the gift of God is eternal life in Jesus Christ our Lord" (Romans 6:23). God brought Jesus back from the dead. He provided the way for you to have a personal relationship with Him through Jesus. Trust Him. Pursue Him.

When we realize how deeply our sin grieves the heart of God and how desperately we need a Savior, we are ready to receive God's offer of salvation. To admit we are sinners means turning away from our sin and selfishness and turning to follow Jesus. The Bible word for this is "repentance"—to change our thinking to acknowledge how grievous sin is, so our thinking is in line with God's.

All that's left for you to do is to accept the gift that Jesus is holding out for you right now: "If you confess with your mouth,

'Jesus is Lord,' and believe in your heart that God raised him from the dead, you will be saved. For it is with your heart that you believe and are justified, and it is with your mouth that you confess and are saved" (Romans 10:9–10). God says that if you believe in His son, Jesus, you can live forever with Him in glory: "For God so loved the world that He gave his one and only Son, that whoever believes in him shall not perish, but have eternal life" (John 3:16).

Are you ready to accept the gift of eternal life that Jesus is offering you right now? Let's review what this commitment involves:

- I acknowledge I am a sinner in need of a Savior. I repent or turn away from my sin.
- I believe in my heart that God raised Jesus from the dead. I trust that Jesus paid the full penalty for my sins.
- I confess Jesus as my Lord and my God. I surrender control of my life to Jesus.
- I trust Jesus as my Savior forever. I accept that God has done for me what I could never do for myself when He forgives my sins.

If it is your sincere desire to receive Jesus into your heart as your personal Lord and Savior, then talk to God from your heart. Here's a suggested prayer:

> *Lord Jesus, I know that I am a sinner and I do not deserve eternal life. But, I believe You died and rose from the grave to make me a new creation and to prepare me to dwell in your presence forever. Jesus, come into my life, take control of my life, forgive my sins and save me. I am now placing my trust in You alone for my salvation and I accept your free gift of eternal life.*

If you've prayed this prayer, it's important that you take these three next steps: First, go tell another Christian! Second, get plugged into a local church. Third, begin reading your Bible every day (we suggest starting with the book of John). Welcome to God's forever family!

Endnotes

[1] See 2 Peter 3:6; Genesis 1; and Romans 8:22.
[2] See Romans 5:12 and 1 Corinthians 15:22.
[3] Dr. Andrew A. Snelling, "Noah's Lost World," (May 3, 2015) (*www.answersingenesis.org/geology/plate-tectonics/noahs-lost-world/*) (January 26, 2017).
[4] *The New Defender Study Bible* (Nashville, TN: World Publishing, 2006) states, "9:13 my bow. The rainbow, requiring small water droplets in the air, could not form in the pre-diluvian world, where the high vapor canopy precluded rain (Genesis 2:5). After the Flood, the very fact that rainfall is now possible makes a worldwide rainstorm impossible, and the rainbow "in the cloud" thereby becomes a perpetual reminder of God's grace, even in judgment." Several other Biblical Creation resources hold this view.
[5] Catherine Brahic, *New Scientist Daily News* (April 24, 2007). "Mystery prehistoric fossil verified as giant fungus": (*www.newscientist.com/article/dn11701-mystery-prehistoric-fossil-verified-as-giant-fungus/#.Uea7Qo2G18E*) (January 26, 2017).
[6] *Guinness World Book of Records 2014*, (The Jim Pattison Group, 2014): 27.
[7] Image Credit: Wikipedia.
[8] Gregory S. Paul, *Dinosaurs of the Air: The Evolution and Loss of Flight in Dinosaurs and Birds* (Johns Hopkins University Press, 2002): 472. See also: M.P. Witton and M.B. Habib. "On the Size and Flight Diversity of Giant Pterosaurs, the Use of Birds as Pterosaur Analogues and Comments on Pterosaur Flightlessness." *PLoS ONE*, 5(11) (2010). Other estimates place a range the weight range between 440 and 570 pounds: "That said, most mass estimates for the largest pterosaurs do converge, using multiple methods, around a 200–260kg (440–570lb) range at present, which represents decent confidence." (Ella Davies, BBC Earth, May 9, 2016) and "The biggest beast that ever flew had wings longer than a bus." (*www.bbc.com/earth/story/20160506-the-biggest-animals-that-ever-flew-are-long-extinct*) (January 26, 2017).
[9] Larry O' Hanlon, November 8, 2012. "This pterodactyl was so big it couldn't fly, scientist claims." *www.nbcnews.com/id/49746642/ns/technology_and_science-science/#.WH-U2_krKUn* (January 26, 2017).
[10] Mark P. Wilton, *Pterosaurs: Natural History, Evolution, Anatomy.* (Princeton University Press, 2013).
[11] Ian Anderson, "Dinosaurs Breathed Air Rich in Oxygen," *New Scientist*, vol. 116, 1987, p. 25.
[12] Image Credit: Wikipedia.
[13] "No giants today: tracheal oxygen supply to the legs limits beetle size," was presented October 10–11 at Comparative Physiology 2006: Integrating Diversity (Virginia Beach). The research was carried out by Alexander Kaiser and Michael C. Quinlan of Midwestern University, Glendale, Arizona; J. Jake Socha and Wah-Keat Lee, Argonne National Laboratory, Argonne, IL; and Jaco Klok and Jon F. Harrison, Arizona State University, Tempe, AZ. Harrison is the principal investigator.
[14] Geological Society of America. "Raising giant insects to unravel ancient oxygen." *Science Daily*, October 30, 2010. *www.sciencedaily.com/releases/2010/10/101029132924.htm* (January 26, 2017). See also: Gauthier Chapelle & Lloyd S. Peck (May 1999). "Polar

gigantism dictated by oxygen availability." *Nature.* 399 (6732): 114–115. This article argues that higher oxygen supply (30–35%) may also have led to larger insects during the Carboniferous period: A.N. Nel, G. Fleck, R. Garrouste, and G. Gand, "The Odonatoptera of the Late Permian Lodève Basin (Insecta)." *Journal of Iberian Geology* 34 (1) (2008): 115–122.

[15] Colin Schultz, "Long Before Trees Overtook the Land, Earth Was Covered by Giant Mushrooms," Smithsonian.com (July 17, 2013). *www.smithsonianmag.com/smart-news/long-before-trees-overtook-the-land-earth-was-covered-by-giant-mushrooms-13709647/* (January 26, 2017).

[16] University of Chicago News Office. "Prehistoric mystery organism verified as giant fungus 'Humongous fungus' towered over all life on land" *www.news.uchicago.edu/releases/07/070423.fungus.shtml* (April 23, 2007) (January 26, 2017).

[17] Simon J. Braddy, Markus Poschmann, and O. Erik Tetlie, "Giant claw reveals the largest ever arthropod," *Biological Letters.* (2008) 4 106–109 (Published February 23, 2008).

[18] M. G. Lockley & Christian Meyer. "The tradition of tracking dinosaurs in Europe," *Dinosaur Tracks and Other Fossil Footprints of Europe.* (Columbia University Press, 2013), pp. 25–52. See also: Donald R. Prothero, *Bringing Fossils to Life: An Introduction to Paleobiology.* Third Edition. (New York: Columbia University Press, 2015), p. 381.

[19] See, for example: Rodger Young, "Ussher, Explained and Corrected." *Bible and Spade,* 31 (2) (2018): 45; Brian Thomas, "Two date range options for Noah's Flood," Journal of Creation 31(1) (2017); Henry B. Smith Jr., "Methuselah's Begetting Age in Genesis 5:25 and the Primeval Chronology of the Septuagint: A Closer Look at the Textual and Historical Evidence," Answers Research Journal 10 (2017): 169–179. Answers in Genesis: *www.answersingenesis.org/arj/v10/methuselah-primeval-chronology-septuagint.pdf* (November 5, 2018); and Lita Cosner and Robert Carter, "Textual Traditions and Biblical Chronology," Journal of Creation 29 (2) 2015. Journal of Creation: *www.creation.com/images/pdfs/tj/j29_2/j29_2_99-105.pdf* (November 5, 2018).

[20] Bodie Hodge, "Biblical Overview of the Flood Timeline." (August 23, 2010). Answers in Genesis. *www.answersingenesis.org/bible-timeline/biblical-overview-of-the-flood-timeline/* (December 16, 2021).

[21] Answers in Genesis: "Putting the Ark into Perspective" (January 23, 2014): *www.answersingenesis.org/noahs-ark/putting-the-ark-into-perspective/* (December 16, 2021).

[22] Michael Belknap and Tim Chaffey, "How Could All the Animals Fit on the Ark?" (April 2, 2019): *www.answersingenesis.org/noahs-ark/how-could-all-animals-fit-ark/* (December 16, 2021).

[23] John Woodmorappe, "Chapter 5: How Could Noah Fit the Animals on the Ark and Care for Them? (October 15, 2013; last featured March 2, 2014): *www.answersingenesis.org/noahs-ark/how-could-noah-fit-the-animals-on-the-ark-and-care-for-them/* (December 16, 2021).

[24] Dr. Hong earned his Ph.D. degree in applied mechanics from the University of Michigan, Ann Arbor.

[25] S.W. Hong, S. S. Na, B.S. Hyun, S.Y. Hong, D.S. Gong, K.J. Kang, S.H. Suh, K.H. Lee, & Y.G. Je, "Safety investigation of Noah's Ark in a seaway,"

Creation.com: *www.creation.com/safety-investigation-of-noahs-ark-in-a-seaway* (January 1, 2014).

[26] John Whitcomb, *The World that Perished* (Grand Rapids, Michigan: Baker Book House, 1988): 24.

[27] Y. Eyüp Özveren Shipbuilding, 1590–1790, Vol. 23, No. 1, Commodity Chains in the World-Economy, 1590–1790 (2000), 15–86.

[28] These estimates are based on the smaller cubit size.

[29] Answers in Genesis: Created Kinds (Baraminology): *www.answersingenesis.org/creation-science/baraminology/*

[30] R. M. Nowak, *Walker's Mammals of the World* (6th ed. 2 Vols, Baltimore, Maryland: The Johns Hopkins University Press (1999).

[31] Wilson & Reeder, *Mammal Species of the World* (3rd ed. 2005).

[32] Jean K. Lightner, "Mammalian Ark Kinds," *Answers Research Journal* 5 (2012):151–204. Answers in Genesis: *www.answersingenesis.org/arj/v5/mammalian-ark-kinds.pdf* (November 5, 2018).

[33] Dr. Nathaniel T. Jeanson, "Which Animals Were on the Ark with Noah? Stepping Back in Time." (May 28, 2016) Answers in Genesis: *www.answersingenesis.org/creation-science/baraminology/which-animals-were-on-the-ark-with-noah/* (November 5, 2018).

[34] Ronald J. Litwin, Robert E. Weems, and Thomas R. Holtz, Jr. *Dinosaurs Fact and Fiction* (*www.pubs.usgs.gov/gip/dinosaurs/types.html* and *www.pubs.usgs.gov/gip/dinosaurs/* (November 5, 2018).

[35] World History Encyclopedia. *Enuma Elish - The Babylonian Epic of Creation.* *www.ancient.eu/article/225/enuma-elish---the-babylonian-epic-of-creation---fu/* (December 16, 2021).

[36] Archaeology. *Cuneiform Tablet Tells Giant Ark Story.* *www.archaeology.org/news/1763-140127-ark-cuneiform-translation. (December 16, 2021).*

[37] See for example Sumerian King List. Wikipedia.com *www.en.wikipedia.org/wiki/Sumerian_King_List*

[38] See for example Atra-Hasis. Wikipedia.com *www.en.wikipedia.org/wiki/Atra-Hasis*

[39] See for example Sumerian Creation Myth. Wikipedia.com *www.en.wikipedia.org/wiki/Sumerian_creation_myth*

[40] Frank Lorey, The Flood of Noah and the Flood of Gilgamesh (March 1, 1997): *www.icr.org/article/noah-flood-gilgamesh/*

[41] Gotquestions.org: *www.gotquestions.org/Noahs-ark-questions.html*; Ark Encounter, "How Long for Noah to Build the Ark?" (November 18, 2011): *www.arkencounter.com/blog/2011/11/18/how-long-for-noah-to-build-the-ark/*; Verse by Verse Ministry: *www.versebyverseministry.org/bible-answers/how-long-did-noah-take-to-build-the-ark*; Bodie Hodge, "How Long Did It Take for Noah to Build the Ark?" (June 1, 2010; last featured May 23, 2018): *www.answersingenesis.org/bible-timeline/how-long-did-it-take-for-noah-to-build-the-ark/*

[42] Previous similar versions (in fragmentary form) exist that have been dated earlier.

[43] Jeffrey H. Tigay, "The Evolution of the Gilgamesh Epic," University of Pennsylvania Press, Philadelphia, 1982, 220, 225.

[44] F. Lorey. "The Flood of Noah and the Flood of Gilgamesh." March 1, 1997. *www.icr.org/article/noah-flood-gilgamesh/* (December 16, 2021).

[45] Nick Liguori, *Echoes of Ararat: A Collection of Over 300 Flood Legends from North and South America* (Master Books, 2021): 277 online version.

[46] Liguori, personal communication, December 12, 2021.

[47] James J. S. Johnson, "Genesis in Chinese Pictographs." Institute for Creation Research. February 27, 2015. *www.icr.org/article/genesis-chinese-pictographs/* (December 16, 2021).

[48] Sharon Turner, The Sacred History of the World, vol. 2 (London: Longman, 1834), pp. 324-325.

[49] Robert Morrison, A Dictionary of the Chinese Language, In Three Parts, vol. 1 (Macao: East India Company Press, 1815), p. xiv. Turner adds (p. 324): "The Han-lin commentators on the Chou-king and Houn-gan-koue remark, that this deluge did not happen in the time of Yao, but before him. The text of the Tchin-tsee, and the commentary of the Tehun-meou, are cited on this point in the Dissertation written by Ko, a Chinese, prefixed to Mémoirs des Chinoise, vol. 1, p. 159."

[50] Lo-pi, author of the Lu-shi, as quoted in: Joseph Marie Amiot, François Bourgeois, et al, Mémoirs des Chinoise, vol. 1 (Paris: Nyon, 1776), p. 157.

[51] Mémoirs des Chinoise, vol. 1, p. 158.

[52] Ibid., p. 159.

[53] Ibid.

[54] James Legge, The Chinese Classics, vol. 3, part 1 (London: Trubner & Co., 1865), p. 76.

[55] Samuel Clarke writes: "They have plenty of legends handed down from earlier times. Who composed these legends no one knows; they are taught by the older people to the girls and boys. Many of them are in verse, five syllables to a line, the stanzas being of unequal length, one stanza interrogative and one responsive. These are sung or recited at their festivals by two persons or two groups, generally one group of young men and one group of young women. Among the Tribes of South-west China (London: Morgan & Scott, 1911), p. 49.

[56] Edgar A. Truax, "Genesis According to the Miao People," Acts and Facts, vol. 20, no. 4 (San Diego: Institute for Creation Research, 1991).

[57] Ibid.

[58] Ibid.

[59] Samuel Clarke, Among the Tribes in South-west China (London: Morgan & Scott, 1911), p. 130.

[60] John White, *The Ancient History of the Maori,* vol. 1 (Wellington: George Disbury, 1887), pp. 172-180.

[61] "Plate Tectonics: Shaping the Continents." *California Academy of Sciences.* www.calacademy.org/explore-science/plate-tectonics-shaping-the-continents. (September 22, 2020).

[62] Image credit: Dr. John Baumgardner.

[63] Answers in Depth, Vol. 5 (2010). *www.answersingenesis.org/doc/articles/aid/v5/catastrophic_plate_tectonics.pdf* (November 5, 2018).

[64] See: "Noah's Flood and Catastrophic Plate Tectonics (from Pangea to Today)." Posted July 20, 2018. *Genesis Apologetics. https://youtu.be/zd5-dHxOQhg.* Accessed September 22, 2020.

[65] Steve Austin, "Continental Sprint: A Global Flood Model for Earth History - Dr. Steve Austin (Conf Lecture)." Posted February 20, 2019. *Is Genesis History? www.youtu.be/0RLlbUBpzr0.* (September 22, 2020).
[66] Chandler Burr, "The Geophysics of God: A scientist embraces plate tectonics—and Noah's flood." *U.S. News & World Report.* Archived from the original on August 10, 2007 (Original published June 8, 1997): pp. 55–8.
[67] Thanks to Dr. John Baumgardner for contributing this section (personal communication, May 21, 2018).
[68] Plate Tectonics Theory, National Park Service: for Teachers Scalera, Giancarlo. "Roberto Mantovani (1854–1933) and his ideas on the expanding Earth, as revealed by his correspondence and manuscripts." *Annals of Geophysics* 52 (6) (December 2, 2009): 617.
[69] Earth bathymetry by AlteredQualia (Data from NASA Blue Marble). *AlteredQualia.com. www.alteredqualia.com/xg/examples/earth_bathymetry.html.* (September 22, 2020).
[70] Atlantic Ocean Floor. *National Geographic Magazine* (June, 1968).
[71] "Ring of Fire." USGS. July 24, 2012. Retrieved June 13, 2013; "Where do earthquakes occur?" USGS. May 13, 2013. Archived from the original on August 5, 2014. Retrieved June 13, 2013.
[72] Image credit: Wikipedia.
[73] S. H. Kirby, (1983) "Rheology of the lithosphere," *Reviews of Geophysics and Space Physics* 25, 1219–1244.
[74] J. R. Baumgardner, (2003) "Catastrophic plate tectonics: the physics behind the Genesis Flood," in *Proceedings of the Fifth International Conference on Creationism,* R. L. Ivey, Jr., Editor, Creation Science Fellowship, Pittsburgh, PA, 113–126.
[75] Baumgardner, 2018.
[76] J. R. Baumgardner (2018). Understanding how the Flood sediment record was formed: The role of large tsunamis. In *Proceedings of the Eighth International Conference on Creationism,* ed. J.H. Whitmore, 287–305. Pittsburgh, Pennsylvania: Creation Science Fellowship.
[77] Ibid.
[78] Ibid.
[79] J. R. Baumgardner, (2018). "The Importance of the Genesis Flood to a Correct Understanding of the Earth's Past" (PowerPoint Presentation).
[80] Image credit: John D Morris, *The Global Flood: Unlocking Earth's Geologic History.* Dallas, TX: Institute for Creation Research. 2012.
[81] Carl Werner, "Evolution the Grand Experiment," The Grand Experiment: *www.thegrandexperiment.com/index.html* (January 1, 2014).
[82] There is disagreement in the paleontology field as to whether the "dinosaur death pose" is due to choking while dying from drowning, or due to strong water currents arching the neck back after death. See: Reisdorf, Achim G. & Wuttke, Michael. "Re-evaluating Moodie's Opisthotonic-Posture Hypothesis in Fossil Vertebrates Part I: Reptiles—the taphonomy of the bipedal dinosaurs *Compsognathus longipes* and *Juravenator starki* from the Solnhofen Archipelago (Jurassic, Germany)," *Palaeobiodiversity and Palaeoenvironments* 92 (2012): 119–168.
[83] Liu, L., Spasojevi, S. & Gurnis, M. (2008), Reconstructing Farallon Plate Subduction Beneath North America back to the Late Cretaceous, *Science,*

322, 934–938; Spasojevi, S., Liu, L. & Gurnis, M. "Adjoint Convection Models of North America Incorporating Tomographic, Plate motion and Stratigraphic Constraints." *Geochem., Geophy., Geosys* 10 (2009) Q05W02; Bond, Gerard. "Evidence for continental subsidence in North America during the Late Cretaceous global submergence." *Geology* 4 (9) (September 1, 1976): 557–560; Cross, Timothy A. & Pilger, Rex H. Jr. "Tectonic controls of late Cretaceous sedimentation, western interior, USA." *Nature*, Volume 274, 653–657 (1978).

[84] Thanks to Dr. John Baumgardner for contributing this section (personal communication, May 21, 2018).

[85] Data from the Paleobiology Database: *www.paleobiodb.org/navigator/*. (January 26, 2017).

[86] Image credit: Tom Vail, "Bent Rocks." Posted December 8, 2015. *Canyon Ministries. www.canyonministries.org/bent-rock-layers/*. (September 22, 2020).

[87] See also: Ken Ham, "Too Little Sediment" (Series: 10 Best Evidences for a Young Earth) (January 17, 2022). *www.answersingenesis.org/media/audio/answers-with-ken-ham/volume-144/too-little-sediment*

[88] T.L. Clarey & D.J. Werner, "Use of sedimentary megasequences to re-create pre-Flood geography." In *Proceedings of the Eighth International Conference on Creationism*, ed. J.H. Whitmore, (2018): pp. 351–372. Pittsburgh, Pennsylvania: Creation Science Fellowship. Note: the literature on this topic reports 1,500 bore holes, but this has since increased to 2,000.

[89] Courtesy of Dr. Nathaniel Jeanson.

[90] Image credit: T. Clarey & D. J. Werner (2018).

[91] Andrew Snelling, "How Did We Get All This Coal?" Posted April 1, 2013. *Answers in Genesis. www.answersingenesis.org/biology/plants/how-did-we-get-all-this-coal/*. (September 22, 2020).

[92] Map courtesy of Lignite Energy Counsel.

[93] The Paleobiology Database (Frequently Asked Questions): *www.paleobiodb.org/#/faq*. (January 26, 2017).

[94] The Paleobiology Database: *www.paleobiodb.org/navigator/*. (January 26, 2017).

[95] RATE tested the assumptions using radiohalos and fission tracks. Both showed that the assumptions were violated (Vardiman, Larry et al., *Radioisotopes and the Age of the Earth: Results of a Young-Earth Research Initiative*. The Institute for Creation Research, December 1, 2000).

[96] Ken Ham, "They Can't Allow 'It'!" Posted August 1, 2005. Answers in Genesis. *www.answersingenesis.org/the-flood/global/they-cant-allow-it/*. Accessed September 22, 2020.

[97] Edgar Blake, "Dinosaur National Monument." *Dinosaur Digs*. Bethesda, MD: Discovery Communications, 1999: p. 120.

[98] An articulated dinosaur skeleton means that a large number of the bones from an individual dinosaur were collected in close association, enough to reassemble the dinosaur.

[99] Carl Werner, *Evolution: The Grand Experiment* (Vol. 1), Kindle Locations 2598–2608.

[100] See endnote above about the disagreement in the paleontology field as to whether the "dinosaur death pose" is due to choking while dying from drowning, or due to strong water currents arching the neck back after death..

[101] The Paleobiology Database: *www.paleobiodb.org/navigator/*. (January 26, 2017).

[102] Eberth, D.A., Brinkman, D.B., and Barkas, V.A. "Centrosaurine Mega-bonebed from the Upper Cretaceous of Southern Alberta: Implications for Behaviour and Death Events" in *New Perspectives on Horned Dinosaurs: The Ceratopsian Symposium at the Royal Tyrrell Museum* (September 2007).
[103] *New Perspectives on Horned Dinosaurs: The Ceratopsian Symposium at the Royal Tyrrell Museum* (September 2007).
[104] Other researchers have framed similar explanations about the same area: "It looks like catastrophe… We think a herd was trying to cross a river in flood. These animals weren't too bright." Phillip Currie, quoted in Rick Gore, "Dinosaurs." *National Geographic* (January, 1993): p. 46.
[105] Carl Werner, *Evolution: The Grand Experiment* (Vol. 1), Kindle Locations 2598–2608.
[106] Michael Reilly, "Dinosaurs' Last Stand Found in China?" *Discovery.com*. www.news.discovery.com/earth/dinosaurs-last-stand-found-in-china.htm. Janu(ary 1, 2014).
[107] Michael Oard, "The Extinction of the Dinosaurs," *Journal of Creation* 11(2) (1997): 137–154.
[108] Horner, J.R. & Gorman, J. *Digging Dinosaurs*. New York: Workman Publishing, 1988: 122–123.
[109] Credit: Caleb LePore. See: Braun, David. "Dinosaur Herd Found in Canada Named After Science Teacher." *National Geographic News*. National Geographic Society, October 2, 2008; Brochu, Christopher A., Brett-Surman, M. K. "Dinosaur Provincial Park." *A Guide to Dinosaurs*. San Francisco, CA: Fog City, 2002: p. 220; Horner, John R. & Gorman, James. *Digging Dinosaurs*. New York: Workman Pub., 1988: p. 131; French, Brett. "New Finds, Old Site: Dinosaur Dig Revealing Insights into Montana 103 Million Years Ago." *Butte Montana Local News*. August 23, 2015; French, Brett, "Jurassic Starfish Discovery in South-central Montana Wows Researchers." *Independent Record*. July 6, 2015; Edgar, Blake. "Petrified Forest National Park." *Dinosaur Digs*. Bethesda, MD: Discovery Communications, 1999: p. 104; Glendive Dinosaur and Fossil Museum, Glendive, Montana; Dunham, Mike. "Scientists Identify Dinosaur That Roamed the Alaska Arctic." *Alaska Dispatch News*. Alaska Dispatch Publishing. September 22, 2015.
[110] "Living Fossils Display No Signs of Evolution's Long Ages." *Institute for Creation Research*. www.icr.org/living-fossils/. (September 22, 2020).
[111] Philip John Currie (who helped found the Royal Tyrrell Museum of Paleontology in Drumheller, Alberta), stated: "Bones do not have to be 'turned into stone' to be fossils, and usually most of the original bone is still present in a dinosaur fossil." (Currie, P.J. & Koppelhus, E.B. *101 Questions about Dinosaurs*. Dover Publications, 1996: p. 11.
[112] Jeff Hecht, "Blood vessels recovered from *T. rex* bone." March 24, 2005. NewScientist.com (Daily News). *www.newscientist.com/article/dn7195-blood-vessels-recovered-from-t-rex-bone/*. (September 22, 2020).
[113] Science via AP, www.msnbc.msn.com/id/7285683/. (January 27, 2017).
[114] See, for example: Pawlicki, R. & Wowogrodzka-Zagorska, M. "Blood vessels and red blood cells preserved in dinosaur bones." *Annals of Anatomy* 180 (1998): 73–77; Schweitzer, M. H., Wittmeyer, J.L., Horner, J.R., and Toporske, J.K. "Soft-tissue vessels and cellular preservation in *Tyrannosaurus rex*." *Science,* 307 (2005): 1952; Schweitzer M.H., Wittmeyer, J.L., and Horner, J.R. "Soft tissue and cellular

preservation in vertebrate skeletal elements from the Cretaceous to the present." *Proceedings of the Royal Society B* 274 (2007): 183–197; Schweitzer, M.H., Zheng, W., Organ, C.L., Avci, R., Suo, Z., Freimark, L.M., Lebleu, V.S., Duncan, M.B., Vander Heiden, M.G., Neveu, J.M., Lane, W.S., Cottrell, J.S., Horner, J.R., Cantley, L.C., Kalluri, R., and Asara, J.M. "Biomolecular characterization and protein sequences of the campanian Hadrosaur B. *Canadensis*." *Science*, 324 (2009): 626–631.

[115] Schweitzer, M. & Staedter, I. *The Real Jurassic Park, Earth*, June 1997, pp. 55–57.

[116] See next reference. These two images are from a 2005 discovery from Dr. Schweitzer that clearly show blood vessels from a T. rex bone.

[117] Pawlicki, R. and Wowogrodzka-Zagorska, M. "Blood vessels and red blood cells preserved in dinosaur bones." *Annals of Anatomy* 180 (1998): 73–77; Schweitzer, et al., 2005, 1952; Schweitzer, et al., 2007, 183–197; Schweitzer, et al., 2009, 626–631; Lindgren, J., Caldwell, M.W., Konishi, T., Chiappe, L.M., "Convergent Evolution in Aquatic Tetrapods: Insights from an Exceptional Fossil Mosasaur." *PLoS ONE* 5 (8) (2010): e11998.

[118] Yeoman, Barry, "Schweitzer's Dangerous Discovery." Posted April 27, 2006. *Discovery Magazine*. www.discovermagazine.com/2006/apr/dinosaur-dna. Accessed January 27, 2017.

[119] Schweitzer, M.H., Marhsall, M., Carron, K., Bohle, D.S., Busse, S.C., Arnold, E.V., Barnard, D., Horner, J.R., and Starkey, J.R. "Heme compounds in dinosaur trabecular bone." *Proceedings of the National Academy of Sciences* USA 94, (1997): p. 6295.

[120] Asara, J.M., Schweitzer, M.H., Freimark, L.M., Phillips, M., and Cantley, L.C. "Protein sequences from mastodon and Tyrannosaurus rex revealed by mass spectrometry." *Science*, 316 (2007): 280–285.

[121] Armitage, M., "Soft bone material from a brow horn of a *Triceratops horridus* from Hell Creek Formation, MT." *Creation Research Society Quarterly*, 51 (2015): 248–258.

[122] Schweitzer, M.H., Zheng, W., Cleland, T.P., and Bern, M. "Molecular analyses of dinosaur osteocytes support the presence of endogenous molecules." *Bone*, 52 (2013): 414–423; Armitage, 2015, 248–258; Armitage, M. and Anderson, K.L. "Soft tissue of fibrillar bone from a fossil of the supraorbital horn of the dinosaur *Triceratops horridus*." *Acta Histochemica*, 115 (2013): 603–608; Pawlicki, R., "Histochemical demonstration of DNA in osteocytes from dinosaur bones." *Folia Histochemica Et Cytobiologica*, 33 (1995): 183–186.

[123] M.H. Schweitzer, et al. 2005. "Molecular preservation in Late Cretaceous sauropod dinosaur eggshells." *Proceedings of the Royal Society B: Biological Sciences*. 272 (1565): 775–784.

[124] Cody, G.D., Gupta, N.S., Briggs, D.E.G., Kilcoyne, A.L.D., Summons, R.E., Kenig, F., Plotnick, R.E., and Scott, A. C. "Molecular signature of chitin-protein complex in Paleozoic arthropods." *Geology*, 39 (3) (2011): 255–258; Ehrlich, H., Rigby, J.K., Botting, J.P., Tsurkan, M.V., Werner, C., Schwille, P., Petrášek, Z., Pisera, A., Simon, P., Sivkov, V.N., Vyalikh, D.V., Molodtsov, S.L., Kurek, D., Kammer, M., Hunoldt, S., Born, R., D. Stawski, Steinhof, A., Bazhenov, V.V., and Geisler, T. "Discovery of 505-million-year old chitin in the basal demosponge *Vauxia gracilenta*." *Scientific Reports*. 3 (2013): 3497.

[125] Helder, M., "Fresh dinosaur bones found," *Creation* 14 (3) (1992): 16–17, *www.creation.com/fresh-dinosaur-bones-found.* (January 27, 2017).
[126] Joling, Dan. "Fossils of new duck-billed, plant-eating dinosaur species found in Alaska, researchers say." September 25, 2015. *Yukon News. www:accesswdun.com/article/2015/9/337248.*
[127] Schweitzer, Wittmeyer, & Horner (2007), 183–197.
[128] Mori, Hirotsugu, Druckenmiller, Patrick S., and Erickson, Gregory M., "A new Arctic hadrosaurid from the Prince Creek Formation (lower Maastrichtian) of northern Alaska." *Acta Palaeontologica Polonica* 61 (1), (2016): 15–32; Fiorillo, A.R., McCarthy, P.J., and Flaig, P.P. "Taphonomic and sedimentologic interpretations of the dinosaur-bearing Upper Cretaceous Strata of the Prince Creek Formation, Northern Alaska: Insights from an ancient high-latitude terrestrial ecosystem." *Palaeogeography, Palaeoclimatology, Palaeoecology* 295 (2010): 376–388; Gangloff, R.A. & Fiorillo, A.R. "Taphonomy and paleoecology of a bonebed from the Prince Creek Formation, North Slope, Alaska." *Palaios*, 25 (2010): 299–317; Schweitzer, M.H., Johnson, C., Zocco, T.G., Horner, J.R., and Starkey, J.R., "Preservation of biomolecules in cancellous bone of *Tyrannosaurus rex*," *J. Vertebrate paleontology* 17 (2) (1997): 349–359; Schweitzer, M.H., Marshall, M., Carron, K., Bohle, D.S., Busse, S.C., Arnold, E.V., Barnard, D., Horner, J.R., and Starkey, J.R., "Heme compounds in dinosaur trabecular bone," *Proceedings of the National Academy of Science* 94 (1997): 6291–6296; As stated in Helder (above): "An initial announcement was printed in 1985 in Geological Society of America abstract programs Vol.17, p. 548. Already in press at that time was an article describing the site and the condition of the bones (Davies, Kyle L., 'Duck-bill Dinosaurs (Hadrosauridae, Ornithischia) from the North Slope of Alaska', *Journal of Paleontology*, Vol. 61 No.1, pp.198–200); Schweitzer, Wittmeyer, & Horner, 2007, 183–197.
[129] Yeoman, 2006.
[130] Severo Avila, "Alan Stout is the Bone Collector." Posted April 11, 2010. Northwest Georgia News: *www.northwestgeorgianews.com/rome/lifestyles/alan-stout-is-the-bone-collector/article_6b1268e7-3350-5dfd-a3dc-652dcf27d174.html.* (January 27, 2017).
[131] Alan Stout, Personal communication, January 16, 2017.
[132] Bern, Marshall, Phinney, Brett S., and Goldberg, David. "Reanalysis of *Tyrannosaurus Rex* Mass Spectra." *Journal of Proteome Research* 8.9 (2009): 4328–4332.
[133] Brian Thomas, "Original Biomaterials in Fossils." *Creation Research Society Quarterly*, 51 (2015): 234–347.
[134] Schroeter, E. R., Dehart, C. J., Cleland, T. P., Zheng, W., Thomas, P. M., Kelleher, N. L., Bern, M., & Schweitzer, M. H. Expansion for the Brachylophosaurus canadensis Collagen I Sequence and Additional Evidence of the Preservation of Cretaceous Protein. *Journal of Proteome Research*, 16 (2) (2017): 920–932.
[135] Hays, Brooks. "Scientists find ancient dinosaur collagen." Posted January 23, 2017. *Science News. www.upi.com/Science_News/2017/01/23/Scientists-find-ancient-dinosaur-collagen/6091485202598/.* (September 22, 2020).
[136] Bertazzo, S., et al. "Fibres and cellular structures preserved in 75-million-year-old dinosaur specimens," *Nature Communications*, 6, (2015).

[137] Buckley, M. & Collins, M. J. "Collagen survival and its use for species identification in Holocene-Lower Pleistocene bone fragments from British archaeological and paleontological sites." *Antiqua*, 1 (2011): e1.

[138] Service, Robert F. "Scientists retrieve 80-million-year-old dinosaur protein in 'milestone' paper." Posted January 31, 2017. *Science.com*. www.sciencemag.org/news/2017/01/scientists-retrieve-80-million-year-old-dinosaur-protein-milestone-paper. Accessed February 5, 2017.

[139] Schweitzer, et al. *Bone*, 2013, 414–423; Woodward, S. R., Weyand, N. J., and Bunnell, M. "DNA Sequence from Cretaceous Period Bone Fragments." *Science*, 266 (5188) (1994): 1229–1232.

[140] Lingham-Soliar, T. "A unique cross section through the skin of the dinosaur *Psittacosaurus* from China showing a complex fibre architecture." *Proceedings of the Royal Society B: Biological Sciences* 275 (2008): 775–780. Lingham-Soliar, T. and Plodowski, G. "The integument of *Psittacosaurus* from Liaoning Province, China: taphonomy, epidermal patterns and color of a ceratopsian dinosaur." *Naturwissenschaften* 97 (2010): 479–486.

[141] Michael Greshko, "The Amazing Dinosaur Found (Accidentally) by Miners in Canada." Posted November 1, 2017. *National Geographic*. www.nationalgeographic.co.uk/history-and-civilisation/2017/11/amazing-dinosaur-found-accidentally-miners-canada. Accessed September 22, 2020.

[142] Ibid. Photographs by Robert Clark.

[143] Schweitzer, Zheng, Cleland, & Bern (2013): 414–423.

[144] Ibid.

[145] Edwards, N.P., Barden, H.E., van Dongen, B.E., Manning, P.L., Larson, P.O., Bergmann, U., Sellers, W.I., and Wogelius, R.A. "Infrared mapping resolves soft tissue preservation in 50 million year-old reptile skin." *Proceedings of the Royal Society B*, 278 (2011): 3209–3218.

[146] Bergmann, U., et al., "*Archaeopteryx* feathers and bone chemistry fully revealed via synchrotron imaging." *Proceedings of the National Academy of Sciences*. 107 (20) (2010): 9060–9065.

[147] Hayashi, S., Carpenter, K., Watabe, M., and McWhinney, L.A., "Ontogenetic histology of *Stegosaurus* plates and spikes." *Palaeontology* 55 (2012): 145–161.

[148] Schweitzer, M.H., *Science*, 2009, 626–631.

[149] Alida M Bailleul, Wenxia Zheng, John R Horner, Brian K Hall, Casey M Holliday, Mary H Schweitzer, Evidence of proteins, chromosomes and chemical markers of DNA in exceptionally preserved dinosaur cartilage, National Science Review, Volume 7, Issue 4, April 2020, Pages 815–822, www.doi.org/10.1093/nsr/nwz206

[150] Credit: Alida Bailleul and Wenxia Zheng. Science China Press.

[151] Armitage, M. (2021). First Report of Peripheral Nerves in Bone from *Triceratops horridus* Occipital Condyle. Microscopy Today, 29(2), 20-25. doi:10.1017/S1551929521000468

[152] Images by Dinosaur Soft Tissue Research Institute, DSTRI.

[153] See Buckley & Collins, 2011, e1. Hypothetically, if dinosaurs include an unrealistically large mass of initial collagen, it may last as long as 1.7 million years (see Thomas, Brian, "A Review of Original Tissue Fossils and their Age Implications," Proceedings of the Seventh International Conference on Creationism [Pittsburgh, PA: Creation Science Fellowship]). However, this upper estimate assumes that skin, muscles, and connective tissue collagen decays as slowly as bone collagen, which is not typically the case (Brian Thomas, personal communication, February 15, 2017).

[154] Brian Johnson, "Soft tissue preserved in 80-million-year-old dino fossil," Earth Magazine. Posted Thursday, April 30, 2009. *www.earthmagazine.org/article/soft-tissue-preserved-80-million-year-old-dino-fossil.* (September 8, 2020).

[155] Yeoman, 2006.

[156] "Lawsuit: CSUN Scientist Fired After Soft Tissue Found on Dinosaur Fossil." Posted July 24, 2014. *CBSN Los Angeles.* *www.losangeles.cbslocal.com/2014/07/24/scientist-alleges-csun-fired-him-for-discovery-of-soft-tissue-on-dinosaur-fossil/.* (September 22, 2020).

[157] Werner, C. "Evolution the Grand Experiment," The Grand Experiment: *www.thegrandexperiment.com/index.html* (January 1, 2014).

[158] Werner, C. *Living Fossils. Evolution: The Grand Experiment* (Vol. 2). Green Forest, AR: New Leaf Press, 2008, 242.

[159] Brocklehurst, N., Upchurch P., Mannion, P.D., O'Connor, J. The Completeness of the Fossil Record of Mesozoic Birds: Implications for Early Avian Evolution. *PLoS ONE* 7 (6) (2012): e39056. See also: Mitchell, Elizabeth. "Birds Buried with Dinos at K-T Boundary." Posted October 8, 2011. Answers in Genesis. *www.answersingenesis.org/fossils/fossil-record/birds-buried-with-dinos-k-t-boundary/.* (September 22, 2020).

[160] Werner, C. *Evolution: The Grand Experiment* (Vol. 1), Kindle 3458–3459.

[161] Interestingly, the discovering author states, "Moreover, although the tracks may belong to enantiornithine birds, their overall form and size are similar to those of ornithurines (Falk 2011), specifically birds belonging to the modern clade Ardeidae, such as egrets and herons (Elbroch and Marks 2001; Lockley et al. 2009)." (Martin, A.J., Vickers-Rich, P., Rich, T.H. and Hall, M. (2014), Oldest known avian footprints from Australia: Eumeralla Formation (Albian), Dinosaur Cove, Victoria. Palaeontology, 57: 7–19).
See also: Gannon, Megan. "Bird footprints 100 million years old: Oldest ever found in Australia." Posted October 28, 2013. *NBCNEWs.* *www.nbcnews.com/sciencemain/bird-footprints-100-million-years-old-oldest-ever-found-australia-8C11481570.* (September 22, 2020).

[162] Dr. David Weishampel, e-mail communication with Dr. Carl Werner. Cited in Werner, C. *Evolution: The Grand Experiment.* Green Forest, Arkansas: New Leaf Press, 2007, 126.

[163] Creationists debate the nature of the pre-flood world. It is, however, quite possible that it was different in many ways compared to today's world.

[164] Werner, *Evolution: The Grand Experiment* (3rd Edition), Kindle Location 116.

165 Distribution of pterosaur fossil locations. Colored species or genera names correspond to their taxonomic group. Adapted from Witton (Witton, Mark P. *Pterosaurs: Natural History, Evolution, Anatomy*. Princeton University Press (2013). Taxonomic groups based on Unwin et al. (2010) (Unwin, David M. "*Darwinopterus* and its implications for pterosaur phylogeny," in *Acta Geoscientica Sinica*, 31 (1), (2010): 68–69.

166 "Dinosaur Ancestors Alive Earlier than Originally Thought." Posted March 6, 2010. *Answers in Genesis. www.answersingenesis.org/dinosaurs/types/dinosaur-ancestors-alive-earlier/.* (September 22, 2020).

167 Werner, *Evolution: The Grand Experiment* (3rd Edition). New Leaf Press.

168 Lambert, David. *The Encyclopedia of Dinosaurs*. London: Bloomsbury Books, 1994, p. 26–27.

169 Ibid.

170 Werner, Carl. *Evolution: The Grand Experiment*. Green Forest, AR: New Leaf Press, 2007: 86.

171 Chart adapted from: Denton, Michael. *Evolution: A Theory in Crisis*. Bethesda: Adler & Adler, 1985.

172 Charles Darwin, *The Origin of Species by Means of Natural Selection*. New York: The Modern Library, 1859, 124–125.

173 Genesis 10 provides a listing of most of these families. Since not all the family lines are listed in Genesis 10 and a few more are listed in Genesis 11, it's likely that between 78 and 100 language groups were involved.

174 Ibid, Australian Institute of Marine Science (2001) & Lambeck, et al., (2002).

175 Ibid, Cooper, 2018.

176 Paul F. Taylor, "Chapter 11: How Did Animals Spread All Over the World from Where the Ark Landed?" October 18, 2007; last featured February 17, 2014. Answers in Genesis: *www.answersingenesis.org/animal-behavior/migration/how-did-animals-spread-from-where-ark-landed/* (October 24, 2018).

177 It should be noted that different types of vegetation grew back after the Flood based on soil conditions, the different rates of the receding floodwaters in various places, etc.

178 Luis Villazon, "How far can dandelion seeds travel? Make a wish… a dandelion parachute can go further than you would think." *www.sciencefocus.com/nature/how-far-can-dandelion-seeds-travel/* (November 5, 2018).

179 Susan Feldkamp, *Modern Biology* (2006): 618.

180 H. F. Howe & J. Smallwood (1982). "Ecology of Seed Dispersal," *Annual Review of Ecology and Systematics* 13: 201–228.

181 Ginger Allen, "How Did Plants Survive and Disperse after the Flood?" (February 28, 2017). Answers in Genesis: *www.answersingenesis.org/biology/plants/how-did-plants-survive-and-disperse-after-flood/*

Made in the USA
Middletown, DE
30 January 2024